How to Start Your Own Medical Billing Service

Becoming Self-Employed

Gina Thatcher
Smart Billing Solutions

Contents

CHAPTER 1
INTRODUCTION

I start my day just the same as anyone else. I get up, get in the shower, brush my teeth, brush my hair, get dressed, and go to work. The only difference is that I don't set an alarm, I put on my sweats, I don't have a commute, and I don't punch a time clock. For my lunch break, I catch up on my weekly television shows from my DVR with a homemade lunch. My profession is medical billing. I am my own boss, and I work from home.

Today is Sunday. I prepare for the workweek, relaxing and catching up on my e-mail. I plan for my week. I check my calendar for any appointments with physicians or their staff. This week looks pretty open. I finished all my data entry on Friday, so tomorrow I will do some follow-up. Tuesday I will go to all the offices that I work with and collect charge slips and deposits. I will probably go to the grocery store and to the drug store as well.

It is early in the month, so this means that I can take a day off during the week if I choose. I never know when I will receive a novel-size stack of charge slips from Dr. Johnson or two charge slips from Dr. Jones.

In the beginning of the month, there are typically more deposits than charges. Some physicians tend to ignore their charts until the last week of the month, when you inform them that they are at twenty thousand dollars in charges when a normal month is fifty thousand dollars in charges. The deposits then get smaller as the month progresses due to the lack of charges throughout the month. That is when I have to explain, once again, to the physician and/or office manager that the insurance company does not pay the same day or week that a claim is submitted. It can take anywhere from two to six weeks on average, and sometimes even longer, to receive payment on a clean claim.

The last week of the month, I make no plans. I even chose my wedding date so that I would have finished closing my physician's work for the month and that all the patient statements would be sent the week before my wedding. As I said earlier, I am generally slammed with paperwork the last week of the month because the physicians want their numbers to be higher. Not to mention that all the deposits, or stacks of mail, that have sat on the office manager's desk for the last two weeks need to be entered before I can end the month. The zero-dollar-paid claims must be posted. I will send patient statements once I end the month. I want to make sure that I have all the denials and zero-dollar-paid claims data entry completed because the sooner that I get a patient statement out, the sooner the patient can pay it.

You may wonder how I found myself in this field. I actually went to culinary school after high school. But it just wasn't my thing. I left college, moved back in with my parents, and got a job at the local payday loan business. I placed flyers on car windshields and was verbally abused daily by car owners, business owners, and my own regional manager. Needless to say, it was an awful job. Just two doors down from the payday loan business was a sign for a new medical supply business. Weeks later, there was a grand opening celebration. There were electric scooters and wheelchairs galore. I walked in, checked the place out, and recognized a face from another local medical supply store that I had once applied for a job with. This person had told me once before that it was only a family business and that she did not hire outside of the family. A man approached me and introduced himself as the owner. I asked if he was looking for anyone to work for him. He asked about my experience. Of course, my only experience relevant to his business was retail.

The next day, I arrived with my résumé, and within the week, I was hired as a customer care representative. Over the course of a year and a half, I worked in both stores, selling adult diapers, wheelchairs, compression hose, and other various medical supplies. I even delivered and set up medical equipment in people's homes. In between customers (patients), the manager (medical biller) would give me small, tedious medical billing tasks. I copied from old claim forms, making corrections onto new ones on a typewriter. Yes, that's right—a typewriter! Mistakes were out of the question; these were two-part carbon copy claim forms. I filled out forms that were to be sent to physicians for their signatures on medical necessity justification forms, and any other insurance authorization documents. I did filing.

Eventually, I moved to another city and got a job with a medical billing service, working for a man that was obsessed with cats, there were several living in the office. The employees were expected to feed the cats and clean littler boxes. I first worked as a courier, picking up and delivering paperwork to and from numerous physicians' offices. After a short while, I was given a small Medicaid account as my own account to bill for. This job was not for me because of the feline environment and extra duties taking care of them. I was there to be a medical biller. Given my past durable medical equipment (DME) experience at the medical supply store, I soon found a job with a DME supply store specializing in custom wheelchairs. I gained much experience in the field of medical billing working there. Custom wheelchairs have very specific requirements that qualify a patient's insurance to cover them. That is what I did at this job. I was given a patient's name and the wheelchair that best suited them, selected by a specialist in the field. Then I determined whether the insurance company would cover this wheelchair and what information the company needed in order to pay. Getting the information and/or authorization could take weeks, or even months. After I obtained that information, I was done with my part. It then went on to be billed—hopefully paid, but possibly rebilled and maybe even appealed after that.

Denials and appeals are things I knew very little about at this point. I requested training in this area and received some cross-training while I worked there. I then relocated, and my job search was on again. I got a job with a DME store fifty miles from my home. This time, the position I was hired for was very boring, and I was way overqualified. I was on the hunt for another job. I interviewed for an in-house billing position at a general physician's office and got the job. This was my first billing service client. I worked in-house for a little less than a year. I was still commuting an hour each way and one hundred miles a day. I found a local job with the hospital in my town. I went to the physician I was doing in-house billing for and told him that I had gotten another job locally and was going to take it. I then proposed that I still work for him remotely on my own time. I have to admit, I was quite nervous to be giving this doctor an ultimatum. To my surprise and excitement, he went for it. He asked me to write something up that we could agree upon and present it to him. I then worked for the hospital during the day and came home and did the physician billing in the evening. What I used to spend an eight-hour day in the office doing, I now did in only a couple of hours a night. I collected more doctors until I no longer needed the job with the hospital because I was so busy with my medical billing services.

Now don't let my long story of hard work get you down. The reason I am writing this book is so that you can have the knowledge to skip all that stuff. This book is not intended to teach you how to do medical billing itself but to help you gain the knowledge of how to build your business. I have seen the front and back of many professional offices. With this experience, I have collected all the dos and don'ts of being a medical billing service. When I wrote my first contract, I didn't know what I was doing. I wish that I'd had all the knowledge I do today so that I could have avoided some headaches.

Medical billing is not for everyone. It's certainly not a get-rich-quick scheme. You have a lot of learning ahead of you. But once you put in the time and effort to get started and learn, you will find medical billing to be a very economical and rewarding career. The world of medical billing is an ever-changing one. Policies and procedures are constantly being updated.

It takes a pleasant, persistent, strong personality to be in this business. You have to be comfortable interacting with physicians, medical staff, and other healthcare providers, who are typically very serious and intelligent people. You have to be firm with your standards and with your patients.

Medical billing is a profession that will never go away. With all the new technology, some doctors may think that medical billers are a thing of the past. Electronic medical records (EMR) programs provide the physician with laptop computers or tablets to complete his or her chart notes. The provider will complete the superbill (an itemized form consisting of CPT, HCPC, and ICD-9-CM/ICD-10-CM codes) on this laptop. The provider then thinks, *Well, I already did exactly what my biller will do. Why do I need a biller?* But the harsh reality for the provider—and good thing for you and me—is that he or she will always need a biller. The medical insurance companies will do just about anything not to pay the provider. I once sat in on a seminar, and the speaker asked if there was anyone in the room who had ever worked for a health insurance company. One hand in the seminar rose. The speaker asked if it was true that when you processed claims at the insurance company, you were told to open the envelope, put the claim on your desk, and leave it untouched for at least ten days. Her answer was yes. The fact of the matter is that the doctor does not have time to deal with the insurance companies' ridiculous practices.

CHAPTER 2
WHERE TO START

So you've decided to start your own medical billing service, and you don't know where to start. That is why you purchased this book—a great start, indeed! In this chapter, I will discuss the steps you need to take to start your medical billing service.

First things first. What type of billing service will you be? Here is a look at two types of medical billing services:

- Full Medical Billing Service
- Processing Medical Billing Service

Below is a brief description of both of these services so you can decide which service best suits your medical billing business. This book will focus mainly on the full medical billing service, but I would like you to keep in mind there are other service options you can choose from.

Full Medical Billing Service: Probably the most common medical billing service is full medical billing. You will find that this is what most providers are looking for when deciding to use a billing service. This service takes the medical claims from start to finish. Typically, this service charges on a percentage basis. You are responsible for all the coding on the superbill. You must update codes (ICD-9/ICD-10, CPT, and HCPCS) yearly when the new codes are determined. If you are not a certified coder, you cannot code the visit from a provider's dictation; he or she must code it himself onto a superbill. You will input the data from the superbill into the billing software for claims submission to the insurance company, as well as post the explanation of benefits (EOB). If a claim is denied, you must determine whether it is to be rebilled, appealed, billed to the patient, or written off. You will be responsible for billing and collecting patient balances. You must keep up to date on insurance companies' policies and procedures. The services you provide are not restricted, required, or limited by anyone but you. Your contract (see Chapter 4: Contracts) with the provider details what services you will provide.

Processing Medical Billing Service: This medical billing service may be best for someone just starting out in the field. This service requires the minimal amount of time and effort, and there is no liability. The main task of a processing medical billing service is data entry. The typical processing billing service charges per claim form. The billing service receives the superbills from the provider and enters them into the billing software program for claims submission. The superbills are updated by office staff yearly, when codes are updated. You are not responsible for coding. The provider completes the superbills, including procedure and diagnosis codes. You simply enter these codes into your billing software and bill the claim out electronically or on paper. Once these claims are billed out, your job with these claims are done. You will not follow up on these claims or do any patient collections.

You may choose to start a billing service that includes a different combination of services from those described in the full and processing medical billing service.

It is important that you research your choices and medical billing in general. It's always a good idea to network with other people in the industry. You could join an online forum. You should attend insurance seminars or workshops frequently. Medicare and Medicaid host seminars and workshops regularly. Check their websites for dates and locations. While attending these seminars or workshops, meet, converse, and exchange phone numbers and e-mail addresses with as many people as you can. These seminars and workshops are very beneficial. Even before you have clients, you will benefit with the knowledge you take from seminars and workshops and the contacts that you make while you are there. I keep contact information on every medical biller that I meet. Sometimes you just can't figure out what modifier you need to use with your CPT code, maybe a new procedure you know nothing about. There's a good chance another biller you've met knows the answer or knows someone who would. Why not ask your personal physician if he or she is willing to let you in on the office's billing practices—whether they use in-house billers or a billing service, and why. As a medical biller, I often have patients that are inquiring about their bills also ask me about how I got into this business. I am happy to talk to anyone who is interested in becoming a biller. It is a fantastic business to be in!

You may need to take a course on the basics of medical billing before you start your business. Community colleges sometimes offer one-day or weeklong courses on medical billing. You can take an Internet course. You can research the Internet for how to properly complete a claim form. There are many options to learn the basics of medical billing. You must have an understanding of what you are doing. But the real expertise comes from experience—no classroom can teach you that. A class can tell you not to forget to complete Box 31 of the claim form or how to use a code book, but it can't tell you what to do for each denial you will receive. Trust me, you will receive many denials throughout your career, and you will see new ones every week. It takes time to know what to do with each one, and you will learn as you go.

You should choose one or two specialty fields. This is important because you are just starting out. There are many types of providers. Providers can be dentists, chiropractors, therapists, optometrists, DME providers, doctors of hundreds of specialties, family practices, pediatricians, cardiologists, or urologists—just to name a few. The idea of learning all these specialties is overwhelming. After you learn the basics of medical billing, you should then choose what you will specialize in. Once you have a few clients in this specialty, you will feel confident that you understand the billing techniques and may be ready to add a new specialty to your business.

You will need to research and choose a billing software program. You will want to be fully proficient with this software before you start your billing service. I will go more into detail about software in Chapter 6: Choosing Software.

You should establish a basic contract template before you start looking for clients and marketing your medical billing service. Contracts will be discussed in Chapter 4: Contracts.

There are other services that can be offered from your business. Combining a billing service with optional additional services is a good marketing technique and a great way to make more money for your business. You may take a transcribing class and offer a discount to your provider for transcription services in addition to your billing services. This also allows you to audit patient accounts to what you are billing out, which is another service you may offer. Regular internal auditing is the key to being prepared for auditing by insurance companies— not to mention, a requirement of a compliance plan. Current law requires that a compliance plan be in place for all providers who treat Medicare patients. This is not your responsibility as a billing service, but you could offer to do the chart auditing for an additional fee on top of the fees for your billing service. Credentialing is a big part of owning a medical practice. There is a whole industry of companies who do only credentialing. They charge providers to handle all the credentialing issues. Let me tell you, credentialing and completing insurance contracts can be quite a task. They can be very complex and hard to understand. You must be confident in your ability to provide such services. Another service you may offer could be consulting or practice management. You could consult on new practices, such as computer and software installation and training, front office staff training, introducing employee handbooks and policy manuals, organizing a filing system, creating custom templates of patient forms, and creating custom superbills. Practice management may include advising the provider about how to increase revenue. These services are not detailed in this book. If you wish to offer any of these services, I recommend you take the proper steps to become proficient at each skill before you offer it as a charged service to any provider.

There are quite a few preliminary tasks you must get out of the way before you can actually start your business. You must decide on a business structure. This may be a sole proprietorship, a general partnership, a corporation, or a limited liability company (LLC).I recommend consulting an attorney or a CPA about deciding which structure is best for you and your individual circumstances. Whichever structure you choose will then lay out which tasks will follow. You will need to choose a name for your business and get the applicable licenses required by your city and state. This is another thing I suggest consulting an attorney about.

There are several important office supplies you will need before starting your business:

- The number one item you will need is a computer. You will need this to run your software. You may want to research your software first to see what the operating system requirements are before purchasing a new computer. I recommend a computer dedicated solely to business use. You want it to perform fast and for a long time. I find that having a laptop is also a key to a continuing business. You will want to be able to access your database remotely and securely if you are away on vacation. You may want to bring your computer to meetings with providers or seminars you are attending. Having a laptop in this business is very handy. They make all the hardware attachments, too, so you can use it at your home office as well as on the go—no need to have two business computers.

- You will need ICD-9/ICD-10, CPT, and HCPC coding books or the equivalent software for correct coding. Remember, ICD-9/ICD-10 codes are updated annually in October, and CPT and HCPC codes are updated annually in January. You must have the most up-to-date coding references available in order to get your claims paid quickly and accurately.

- You will need a spacious desk and a comfortable chair. After all, you will be spending a lot of time there. Having a slide-out, under-desk keyboard is not only ergonomically correct, but it also leaves you plenty of desk space for you to place your superbills or whatever you are working on right in front of you. It is important to make sure you are not straining your body at your desk. You want to be as ergonomically correct as possible to avoid physical problems down the road.

- You will need a dedicated phone line for patients and your providers to call. However, you should offer the provider multiple contact numbers so he or she can contact you if you are not in the office. Make sure the office knows which numbers are OK to give to patients. You don't want a patient calling your cell phone while you are in the grocery store. If you and your clients reside in different counties or different area codes, it is nice to offer a toll-free line for patients to call. This can be costly and may not be a priority right away. Many telephone companies offer distinctive ring services for a fax number, so you can use one phone line for both speaking and faxing on. But you still have two separate incoming phone numbers for each. There are also a variety of HIPAA-compliant "e-fax" options on the Internet, most of them free of charge. Regardless of how you do it, you should have a fax number available.
- You will need a fax machine even if you have an "e-fax." It may seem dated, but you will find that fax is a common way of sending information to your providers and the insurance companies. I use an all-in-one machine. It is a copy machine, fax machine, printer, and scanner. This is the best deal for your dollar, and you will use all the features of the machine in your business. I use a toner machine instead of an ink jet. The price and efficiency of a toner printer is much more economic for this type of business. You really have no need for a color printer.
- You will need an Internet service. You actually only really need the Internet to transmit claims if you have an internal database software program. This can even be done by dial-up modem. However, you will find it to be very helpful and more efficient to have high-speed Internet, such as digital subscriber line (DSL). Most private insurance companies have websites that you can access real-time information from. You can check eligibility, check claim status, and download

13

explanations of medical benefits. There are plenty of other benefits to having Internet in your office. If you see an abbreviation you are unaware of, you can Google it; if you see a modifier you're not sure you can use, you can Google it; if your provider is referring a patient to a provider you know nothing about, you can Google it. Additionally, products and supplies can be found at excellent prices on the Internet compared with retail stores.

One of my main sources of communication with my providers is e-mail. Providers can be very busy, and e-mail can be one of the easiest and quickest ways for them to get back to you. This will also ensure that you remember to ask the questions you have and to ask them right away. Also, it provides a paper trail for you if the provider does not get back to you in a timely manner or states that you neglected to inform him of certain issues. If an issue is very important, you should always discuss it with your provider directly, in person or over the phone. I always follow up those conversations with an e-mail, going over what was said and making sure everyone is on the same page. This is a great way to show the provider you are on top of the issues and to back yourself up with a paper trail.

- You will need business/productivity software. You will need a word processor such as Microsoft Word for letters to the insurance company, patients, or doctors. Microsoft Excel is excellent spreadsheet software, and I use it all the time. You will need a reliable e-mail program. I prefer Microsoft Outlook, but there is also web-based e-mail to choose from. You'll also need bookkeeping software and a program to invoice providers for your services rendered.
- A backup system is a must-have. If your software is Internet based, then the software provider should have the backup covered; ask to be sure. If you have an internal database, you will need to find another way to

ensure it will be protected with a backup. Make sure you are completing an offsite backup regularly as well.

- You will need a filing cabinet of some sort. I have been at the point where I was working for more doctors at a time that I was prepared for, and I ended up using filing boxes as my cabinet. It is very important that you stay organized. I organize my data entry by date. My billing software program date stamps all my entries. If there is a question about the hard copy, I simply look in my billing software to see what date I entered it into the system. Then I can go to that date in my file cabinet and search for the paper I am looking for. If you or your provider ever has your billing records audited by an insurance company, you will need to be able to provide what they need from you—and quickly. If billing records are audited and you cannot provide them, the insurance company may consider it not to have happened and may recoup money from your provider.

  I organize my file cabinets with letter-size hanging files and manila file folders. Each manila file folder is noted with a physician's name, date, and what the folder contains (e.g., deposits or charges). Each hanging file holds up to several file folders, depending on how much work you did that day. Then when the file cabinet gets full, I archive the oldest paperwork into storage boxes. The hanging files stay in the cabinet, and the manila ones go in the storage box. Label the box, and keep it until you no longer need it. I find it is helpful to keep payments for one year and superbills for about six months. This way, if you need to refer back to something you posted, it is right there with you, and you don't have to go to the provider's office or possibly their storage unit to find it. Once you are done with the files, you will return them to the provider for medical record storage.

- You will need a paper shredder. You cannot simply throw away papers in this business. Anything that contains personal health information, a patient's name, phone number, address, or just about anything and everything you write on that is not kept for medical record *must* be shredded. You will learn more about this in Chapter 9: HIPAA.

- You will need CMS 1500 claim forms and envelopes to send them in. They make windowed envelopes specifically for CMS 1500 claim forms. You can special order these with your return address preprinted on the envelope.

- You will need to find out how your software generates patient statements and if you can print them on plain white paper or if you will need to purchase special statement paper. After you have a provider contracted, you will order statement envelopes. You should find a supplier that works with your statement template. You will need to include return addressed envelopes with the doctor's information on them with the statements. This makes it easier for patients to pay—and you want to make it as easy as possible for patients to pay. You should make the return address on the envelope your own. This way, if there is returned mail, you will get it back quickly and correct and resend it quickly.

- It's a good idea to get a business name and address stamp. You will find that you will use this quite often, unless you have your business name and address preprinted on your envelopes. You may also find it handy and a time saver to get a few other stamps made up. I often use a "faxed" stamp with a date box on it, a "received" stamp with revolving dates, and a "copy" stamp letting you know this page is a copy and you have the original filed away safely. And don't forget a "past due" stamp for those late-paying patients. If your statement doesn't offer a space to pay by credit card, you can get a large stamp made for that with the different types of credit cards to choose from and a place to enter credit card information. Remember, you want to make it easy for them to pay!

- No matter how many providers you work with, if you have more than one, you need to keep them clearly separated from one another. I use stacking letter trays for an "inbox" and have my file cabinets arranged by provider's office to keep me from mixing anyone up. All these things are clearly labeled. Using a color coding system can also help. It would be quite obvious if you had one provider's files mixed up with another's.

And don't forget to make your workspace an inviting environment for yourself. Number one is keeping organized. If you can keep your paperwork where it should be, it should never feel overwhelming. I know that if there is a mess of papers everywhere, I don't know where to start. Personalize your space with pretty artwork. Put family pictures on your desktop and screensavers. It's your space, and you have to be in it every day. Make it what you want it to be!

CHAPTER 3
MARKETING:
GETTING YOUR
FIRST PROVIDER

When planning to market for your first provider, you must first find out what a provider wants from the biller. You may want to do some market research before you start. Conduct interviews with professionals in the field. See if your personal physician or dentist is willing to talk to you about his or her billing practices. Send out a mass mailing letter interview to a group of providers; use a phone book or Google an area map to get a list of physicians. Let the recipient know that you are conducting research and would greatly appreciate input. Make the reply anonymous so they feel comfortable returning it. But also make including his or her name optional. You may note that the office that took the time to review and return your letter may be more inclined to read your mailings in the future and make good potential clients.

There are many different marketing techniques. Try each one and find out what works best for you. Maybe you already know what works best for you, and you are just one step ahead of the game. Using multiple techniques increases your chance of landing more clients. With whatever method you choose, be honest, be prepared, be proactive, and be open-minded, and you can't go wrong.

Advertise your business. Once you have chosen your business name, print up or order business cards. Be sure to include your business name, your name, contact numbers, mailing address, e-mail address, website, and what you do, of course. You may want to get a few dozen printed on magnets. This way, if you leave one with a provider's office, it is useful and gets placed on a file cabinet or refrigerator. If the provider's in-house biller ever gives notice, he may walk past your magnet and contact you to be his next and final biller. Brochures are also effective advertisements. Take a stack to your local hospitals, and ask if you can place them in the physician's break room and/or the cafeteria. Place flyers on the hospital bulletin boards. Remember to return to these locations and refill/repost your advertisements regularly. Frequently changing up your flyers assures they will get noticed. You could attach a coupon, maybe 10 percent off a startup fee. You should also list your business in the yellow pages. You could take out an ad in your local newspaper or a medical publication. These could also have coupons for your services in them. Contact your local medical association to advertise with them, and ask what other medical publications are in your area.

Create a website for your business. There are many webhosts that make creating your own website simple for a great price. You will want to review and update your website frequently so that visitors will know they are getting real and up-to-date information from you.

You may be wondering what you should put in your advertisements. What is necessary; what is not? What is eye-catching? What do providers want to see? This is where your market research becomes essential. Use the information that you gathered to help create advertisements, brochures, and your website. Scope out the competition; see what they are doing. Don't go about it dishonestly—if they ask who you are, you should tell them. Be prepared—if you reveal that you are possible competition, they may not want to talk with you.

When marketing yourself, you will want to put your medical billing knowledge front and center. Some billing services purchase expense software that claims to make anyone proficient at medical billing, but the purchasers don't know the first thing about medical billing. When you meet with a provider for the first time, he or she may ask you lots of questions about billing practices. You will want to know the answers. If you don't, they are likely to disregard you as a potential billing service.

Tell providers what you intend to do for them and their practice. Tell them what makes you stand out above the rest. Tell them your unique qualities; for example, improved cash flow, electronic billing, speedy follow-up on pending or denied claims, patient collections, coding advice, variety of reporting type available, and HIPAA compliancy. Additionally, don't forget to use all the information from your market research to include points that are important to other providers. Remember, the main difference between an in-house biller and a medical billing service to a provider is that the provider's in-house biller is a fixed expense whereas a medical billing service becomes to the provider a variable cost. This will be one of your main selling points to a provider: "If you don't get paid, I don't get paid." (Not necessarily in those words, but you get the point.)

Referrals are definitely a great way to get new business. However, if you are new to the business, this could be difficult as you have no clients. But you should have references in case potential clients ask for them—references that pertain to what you are doing, not your personality. A reference is a person who you worked under that can attest to your work ethic. It would be especially helpful if you ever worked in a medical setting and could use a person that you worked under as a reference. It could be a teacher that you took a pertinent medical billing/business class from. Make sure the teacher knows who you are and believes that you have what it takes to start your own business. After you have a satisfied and secured a client, make sure to ask if he or she would refer you to his or her colleagues. You could offer incentives for referrals; make sure to include this in your advertisements.

As I mentioned in Chapter 2: Where to Start, you should attend seminars and workshops. You can meet valuable people in the field at these seminars. Whenever I attend one, there are usually one or two providers that attend as well. These are the providers that know what they want. Most providers leave seminar attendance to their billers and trust that they will bring back the information that is necessary for the office. Make contact with these providers, tell them who you are, and give them a business card. They may be attending because they are unhappy with their current billing situation and may find your initiative just what they are looking for. Don't forget to mingle with the other billers at the seminar and exchange a few phone numbers for questions that may arise.

Network with people and businesses in your own community. Tell people—friends, coworkers, business associates—that you are starting your own business in medical billing and are currently looking for new clients. Join networking groups such as your local chamber of commerce. Attend their social functions and look for ways to meet the people who are in your target field as well as the ones that work directly with them.

Professional medical societies hold monthly meetings for providers. Generally, these meetings include a business meeting, dinner, and a program. Why not ask the medical society to allow you to be the speaker at that program? You should not go about it as selling your billing service. Offer a program about a topic that all provider types would be interested in, such as patient collection rules and regulations. You could speak about private insurance regulations. Many providers don't know all of the techniques that can be used to collect money from private insurance companies and/or patients. After you have given this presentation, you will find that providers will want to talk to you about your medical billing service. Exchange business cards, and ask the provider for a phone number or e-mail address where you can reach him directly. If you use the office phone number as your main source of communication, you may find that you have a hard time getting a hold of the actual provider. Tell him or her when you will contact him or her to arrange a meeting. Better yet, arrange one right then and there. After all, what are our Smartphones and tablets for?! Some providers might ask you to be a consultant for their office. They may want to hire you to train their staff on your topics of expertise. These are all good ways to get your name and company well known. These are also providers you can use as references. Even if you don't get a billing client right away, your efforts will definitely not be wasted.

Compose a letter introducing yourself and your medical billing service. In the letter, discuss what you do and what benefits a provider would have contracting with your business. Include a business card, flyer, or brochure. Do a mass mailing to local providers. You can use your local yellow pages or find a list of providers by geographical area on the Internet. Mail the letters in stages, as you should make follow-up attempts on each provider you market to. Make sure to make your follow-up calls within a few days. The letters should be to the attention of the office manager. The office manager is generally the one opening and reading the mail. Even if you attention the letter to the provider, the office manager will be the one to read and determine if the provider needs to see it or not. If you initially direct your letter to the office manager, then you will also have a better chance when you follow up to get to speak to the person that opened and read your letter. Ask that person to forward the information to the provider. Even better than a follow-up phone call is a follow-up in person. See if you can meet and discuss your services with the office manager, and then ask to schedule a meeting with the provider himself. Another form of mailings may be a postcard; this is less expensive and can be just as effective. Be sure to mail your letters out on a Monday. This will ensure that they are not received on a Monday, the heaviest mail day. Something that may be seen as junk mail will more likely be disregarded on a Monday. You don't want your mailings to be received on a Friday, either. Office staff tends to be focused on the weekend on a Friday; your mailing may not get the full attention it deserves. Your target receipt date is Tuesday, Wednesday, and Thursday. If you handwrite the name and address on the envelope, it is more likely to be read. If you have a preprinted label stuck on there, it is likely to be seen as a mass mailing and disregarded.

Search the Help Wanted ads in the newspaper or on career websites regularly. If you see an advertisement for a medical biller, you can quickly submit the idea of a medical billing service instead to the provider. You can send a letter or e-mail stating that you saw the advertisement and wanted to make the provider aware of the alternative medical billing services you offer. You can walk into the office, introduce yourself to the office manager, and ask for a meeting with the provider and office manager to discuss your services. Be sure to leave a brochure to review in between then and the meeting. If the ad states specifically how to submit an application or resume, you may follow the same guidelines to contact out of respect of the offices request.

Keep an eye out for new providers in town. Often, new providers are influential when it comes to how their billing could be done. After all, they have nothing to compare it with. Watch for their advertisements in the local papers, and personally meet with them before their new practice doors open up. They may need consulting on practice management as well. You may end up providing more services in the beginning that you normally would with other providers, and it will be well worth it in the end.

As with any business, your clients may come and go. Don't ever stop marketing. You should certainly not take on more than you are capable of, but turning down business is never a good thing. If you become too busy, hire an independent contract laborer to assist you. The downside to hiring an employee is that if you lose a client and no longer need the extra help, then you may find you have to let the employee go. If you contract someone, you can request his or her services when you need them only; there is also less overhead and obligations for an independent contractor.

When you have your first meeting with your first potential client, there are a few things you need to remember. It is a good idea to keep current on the specialty you have chosen. It will impress the provider that you have knowledge and interest in his area of expertise, and it will make your medical billing service stand out among the rest. Research and find out as much as you can about the specific provider you will be meeting with. Additional information regarding the provider can be helpful with your first meeting; you will have an idea of what the provider may be looking for. Does he or she have a high staff/biller turnover? Does he or she already use a medical billing service? Is he or she a member of any IPAs or HMOs? Does he or she accept Medicare and Medicaid? In addition, you can commend him or her on any recent impressive publications or accomplishments he or she has made. You can be more prepared with your presentation when you know more about the provider. Always show up to the meeting on time. Make sure to be confident; never act or look intimidated. It is the provider's job to be a provider, and it is your job to be a biller. Go in confident that you are more knowledgeable about billing than the provider is. The provider needs a biller, and you want him or her to know that you are the billing service that he or she is looking for.

Ask the provider questions, take notes, and ask him or her to ask you any questions. If he has specific billing issues he or she is telling you about, note each one. When he or she is finished describing these issues, offer your thoughts and solutions to each one.

Have copies of sample reports (see Chapter 6: Choosing Software) you can provide to him or her. Let him or her know that you can provide these reports on a monthly or weekly basis. Make him or her feel like he or she is your most important client and that you will treat him or her as such. If your software vendor is capable of creating custom reports, let the provider know that as well. Let the provider know that if he or she is looking for something else in a report, you would be happy to make sure he or she gets exactly what he or she is looking for. Let the provider know that he or she and his or her staff will be able to access real-time information from your database to know whether patients have outstanding balances, their current addresses and phone numbers, their insurance information, and so on. This is why you must know your billing software very well. Know what the benefits are for the provider's office as well as your own.

Providers generally don't have a lot of time. Know that when you do arrange a meeting with a provider, your time will be limited. You want to tell the provider as much as possible in the shortest amount of time. Focus on what you can do for the provider. Don't jump right into your fees; you want him or her to know what you can do for him or her and the practice first and foremost.

If you don't sign an account right away, don't get discouraged. The most difficult part of this business is getting your first client. Just follow the suggestions in this book, and you are sure to land your first client. Also, keep in mind the additional services that can be offered, and market those services to clients that are hesitant or have decided not to go with a medical billing service. This way, you are making some money and getting contacts and exposure. Make friends with your local provider's offices. Visit them frequently. Bring them gifts, such as promotional items like calculators with your business name engraved on them or treats with your logo on them. They will appreciate the gesture, and get to know you better. It may take time for some providers to warm up to the idea of a billing service. Some may not be ready until they lose their in-house biller and are left in a bind. Don't you want to be the first one they call when they find themselves in need of your services? Make sure they know how to get a hold of you!

CHAPTER 4
CONTRACTS

The contract is the most important legal document you must have between you and your provider. It includes what is expected from each party. I strongly advise you to write your contract with an attorney or have an attorney review the contract that you have written. Each state has different laws that you may need to be aware of. You want to make sure that you are protecting your business as well as yourself.

I have worked with quite a few physicians, and let me tell you, less than more know how to run a successful business. Physicians are very intelligent; they go to school for a very long time. Unfortunately, their studies may neglect the knowledge that they will need to run a successful business. I often see physician's spouses in the office, usually in the position of office manager. Things may get touchy when spouses get involved. This is why you need strict and specific policies in your contract to avoid difficult situations. You must enforce abidance of your policies at all times and from the very beginning.

I recommend you take this advice from someone in the field. It is with much time and experience that I have compiled these points to include in your contract. Sometimes, you don't think about things until you are faced with them. It is important to list your expectations as well as address those of the provider. Your contract should include the following.

- Services you will provide, such as:
  - Entering charges from superbill into billing software for claims submission as received from the provider.
  - Coding claims from superbill and maintaining code updates (ICD-9/ICD-10, HCPC, CPT) annually for superbill template.
  - Entering payments into billing software received from insurance and patients.
  - Billing insurance claims to clearinghouses (Chapter 6: Choosing Software) or by paper as necessary.

- o Maintaining patient demographic and insurance information in billing software as received from the office.
- o Making every reasonable attempt to appeal any insurance denial; a list of measures you will take to complete this task is advised.
- o Billing patients' balances as determined by the provider and/or insurance company. It is a good idea to discuss exactly what process you will use (as described in Chapter 8: Insurance Companies and Patient Collections).
- o Returning patient phone calls within a specific timeframe.
- o Noting that patient disputes that cannot be resolved by the biller will be referred to the provider for resolution.
- o Obtaining the provider's paperwork (Chapter 7: Transfer of Paperwork from Provider to You).
- o Performing end of month duties and listing who is responsible for each one.
- o Delivering reports to the provider and explaining when the provider can expect them.
- o Discussing that all superbills, explanations of medical benefits, and any other billing documents will be stored by the billing service until no longer needed for billing purposes, at which time they will be returned to the provider for storage as medical record (the amount of time medical records must be kept by law may vary; check with your local American Medical Association).
- o Discussing that you will be the exclusive billing service for this provider.
- o Explaining how past billings will be handled. Consider this when deciding your startup fee (Chapter 5: Fees) to take on past billing follow-up from the old biller.

31

- Provider responsibilities, such as:
  o How often superbills will be delivered and how many days the superbills have to be completed by the provider from the time that the patient is seen.
  o Information that the provider's office is responsible for gathering and maintaining (for example, patient demographics, insurance cards, etc).
  o How information should be delivered (for example, an Explanation of Medical Benefits should come grouped with a deposit slip or list of checks so the posting can be balanced).
  o What duties the provider has so that you can complete your end-of-month duties when you need to.
  o Completing all insurance contracts and credentialing. Believe it or not, there are people and companies who can be hired to do physician or insurance contracting and credentialing. They get paid well for these services because contracts can be difficult and time consuming. You may want to add this in as a service you provide for an additional fee per contract. If you are up for the challenge that is, make sure you know what you are doing before you agree to complete any insurance contracts or credentialing for your provider.
  o Making "courtesy/bartering adjustments" for patients, most often for other professionals in a similar field. You should have a separate adjustment code for this in your software. State in your contract that the provider will pay you your arranged fee for this adjustment code. You have done the work and should be paid, even if the provider chooses not to be paid or to barter for something for himself or herself.

- o Maintaining patients' signatures on file for assignment of benefits (AOB) forms and HIPAA privacy statements.
- A termination agreement. The termination agreement should be that any party can terminate the contract at any time, with at least thirty days' written notice. I state in my contract that termination can be requested after the initial ninety-day term. I don't want to hold a physician to a contract for any extended period of time. If a client is not happy, you don't want to force that client to keep you as a billing service. I feel that ninety days is a solid amount of time allowed for the provider to see what the billing service can do for the practice. It gives you time to work on the old outstanding claims and accounts and show the provider what you are capable of. It also gives you enough time for an impatient provider that thinks there will be results overnight. Our goal is to get the provider paid as fast as possible, but any biller knows that it inevitably takes time to get paid. Make sure to include an "out" clause; for example, the provider will pay you your regular percentage of 50 percent of the outstanding account receivables on your final closing month as a billing service. This ensures that you get paid for the work that you did that the provider will get paid for after you are no longer the billing service.
- Fees and payments, discussed in detail in Chapter 5: Fees. You will most likely have a desired range of what you *want* to be and are *willing* to be paid for your services. When you arrive at a meeting with a doctor to set up service terms—and fees have not yet been discussed—put your higher percentage on the contract. You can always line through and initial any changes later. Be sure to define any startup fees that you will charge. I assign penalties for provider responsibilities that are not complied with. I also define due date and a finance charge for late payments.

- Notice of time off. You will need to be able to take time off. If you don't plan to have any employees, then you will likely not have anyone to fill in for you. However, it is a good idea to have at least one person trained to help you out in case of a personal emergency or just a longer-than-usual vacation. An acceptable vacation length should not exceed two weeks without someone filling in. Notice of at least one month is customary. If you plan on having children in the future, you may want to include a maternity leave procedure in the contract under this category as well. On a side note, it is a good idea to find out when your provider takes vacations; maybe he goes at the same time every year. It is a good idea to get in your time off when your providers do.
- You will need to have in writing that you are an authorized agency to make calls to the insurance companies and patients on the provider's behalf. This is a HIPAA requirement.
- HIPAA compliance statement. You should include a HIPAA compliance statement in your contract. Make sure you review and comply with all current HIPAA regulations at all times. Here is an example of a HIPAA compliance statement you may include in your contract: *The Contractor warrants and represents that both it and the medical clearinghouse that it uses for the submission of the Company's claims are fully HIPAA compliant. All patient information and data provided by the Company to the Contractor shall be kept confidential and shall not be disclosed to anyone except to the extent necessary for the Contractor to perform its obligations hereunder.*
- Disclaimer. You should always include a disclaimer in your contract. A disclaimer helps protect your business. You should warrant that you are providing true and factual information. The company will warrant the same. If any information is given to you from the company, the company is responsible for the false

information, not you the contractor. Be careful, though—you are responsible for the information that you provide to the patients, insurance companies, and the company as well.

- The last item on the contract will be a signature line and date for both parties. Make sure that if your contract is multiple pages, you include an initial line on all the pages prior to the full signature page. This verifies that you did not make changes on the previous pages after the provider has signed the last page. You will both initial all pages and sign all pages together after you have gone over and agreed on all terms of the contract.

You should always have a basic contract drawn up when you are getting ready to meet with a physician. Depending on the physician and the type of work he or she does, the contract may vary. If your provider is a unique one, such as a midwife or chiropractor, you may want to interview the provider first to find out how things work in the practice. Make the contract unique to the provider.

I like to bring my laptop and a small portable printer to the initial meeting with the doctor to draw up the contract. That way, you can make changes to the contract right then and there and leave your meeting with a signed contract. This can work against you as well, though. It may make it too easy for the provider to make changes to the contract that you may not want to make, like the percentage you will be paid. Changes can always be made at a later time with a pen and both parties' initials. Find out what works well for you and go with it.

CHAPTER 5
FEES

Possibly the most controversial part of starting up your business: what will you charge your clients? It's not like a grocery store, where milk costs $3.50 for everyone, no matter who you are. Each insurance company pays differently according to the contracts in place with the provider, where the practice is located, and many other factors. Some add-on codes are covered by some insurance companies and not others. There are always special circumstances. An average clean claim billed out electronically is paid anywhere from three days to six weeks. Many patients arrange payment plans to pay their balance off over a period of time, of which only about 50 percent or less consistently pay monthly without being constantly reminded by you. It is hard to say how much time and effort you are going to put into an account based on all these factors. You want to make sure that you are going to be fully compensated for the work you will be doing. An office that is primarily Medicaid may try to get a lower percentage because they make less money from the insurance company, though you are doing the same amount of work. An office that has mostly private insurance companies should be able to afford to pay a little more.

The most common pricing methods for medical billing are flat rate per claim pricing or percentage based. You may also choose to charge a monthly flat fee. A new combination method has been on the rise over the last several years due to certain insurance companies in certain states making it illegal for billing services to charge a percentage on money received from these companies. These insurance companies felt it was too easy for the billing service to "upcode" a claim without the provider's knowledge in order to get the insurance company to pay more, increasing the billing service's revenue. This is why it is a good idea to have an attorney review your contract and how you charge your clients. I will explain each pricing method, and you then can decide for yourself which is best suited for your billing service.

First, we will look at the flat fee per claim method. You will base the amount you charge on the actual services you include and the area that you live in. Low charges are based on areas where the cost of living is relatively low, and high charges are based on areas where the cost of living is a bit higher for all the examples given for flat fee per claim method. If you are a straight "processing medical billing service" (described in Chapter 2: Where to Start), then you would probably only charge one to three dollars per claim entered. In this case, all you are doing with these claims is data entry. You are not following up on the claims; follow-up is the responsibility of the provider's office. If you were following up on them, then the fee goes up to about four to seven dollars per claim, regardless of the extent of follow-up. If you sent a clean claim that got paid in two weeks, then you would get paid the same amount for that claim as you would for a claim that you billed out six months ago and are still waiting for the appeals process to commence. Billing services that charge this way may also do so with patient statements, if you agree to make that a part of your services. This fee would probably be one dollar and fifty cents to two dollars and fifty cents per statement sent. When you bill a flat fee per claim method, the upside is that you get paid right away for the work that you have done in that month. You will bill the provider for all the claims and statements that you sent out that month, regardless of whether or not the insurance company or patient has paid the balance.

The flat fee per claim method of charging providers can have several downfalls, primarily from the provider's point of view. There is little to no incentive for the billing service to follow up on a claim. The service has already been paid for the claim and will get nothing more for having to spend extra time on it. It will not be a priority and may just end up being carelessly written off. If follow-up is not included, then the provider must have staff that will do the follow-up. This may defeat the purpose of hiring a billing service to save money on overhead in the first place. The provider will have to have a trained staff member knowledgeable on insurance denials on staff at all times. The same pros and cons are argued for a monthly flat fee.

My recommended method of charging for your services is the percentage-based method if that is legal in your state. You are paid a fixed percentage for any and all money received by the provider for anything that you process. This may or may not include, according to your agreement with the provider, copayments collected at time of service or private pay patients. You could choose to input these payments into the software as a courtesy to the provider, which could also be a selling point of your services. Don't sell yourself short, however; it is a service that you are providing, and you should be paid for it. Don't ever feel obligated to give services away as a courtesy. Sometimes, however, in negotiations with a provider, it may be necessary to secure the account. This is just one example of an incentive for a hesitant provider.

Now, the difficult decision is where to start the percentage at for negotiations. Start with a high number. If you start too low, the provider is not going to tell you that you are selling yourself short and offer you a higher percentage. Negotiations only go down when you throw out the first number. The percentage-based billing method can range from 6 percent to as high as 15 percent, so make sure that you carefully consider and research all the factors that go into determining your percentage.

- First of all, where is the provider located? What is the cost of living? What is the area surrounding the practice like?
- What types of insurance does the provider take? What is the private insurance to Medicaid ratio? Private insurance companies yield more money per claim for the same services (i.e., same amount of claim work) than a Medicaid claim.
- What is the claim volume and average dollar amount? Let's say for example that Provider A has an average of fifty claims per month at an average of one thousand dollars per claim. Provider B has an average claim of one hundred dollars per claim but has on average five hundred claims per month. You would be paid the same

amount of money per month from both providers on average, but Provider B would consist of about ten times more work up front. Thus, you would charge Provider A a lower percentage and Provider B a higher percentage.

- Does the provider use the same codes often that generally get paid right away, making your job easier and percentage lower? If the answer is no, then you have more work to do, and your percentage will be higher.

- Will the provider need additional staff to do follow-up work, which will lower your percentage? Or will you be handling all aspects of billing as described in Chapter 2: Where to Start under "Full Medical Billing Service," which would entitle you to a higher percentage?

- What extra services are you providing? You will need to know how much "extra work" you will be doing. Find out if your provider's claims generally require documentation backup. Does the staff provide you with this right away? Do you have to request it and wait? Does this happen after the initial billing and require an appeals process? Are there secondary and tertiary insurance companies that will need to be billed frequently? Does the staff collect copayments up front, or do you have to bill the patient after the fact? These factors will help you to determine if you need to increase your percentage.

The next thing you will need to consider is a startup fee. With whichever method you choose to bill your clients, you will have extra work getting an account started and should charge a startup fee accordingly. You will be using your own software that you choose, purchase, and pay for yourself (discussed in Chapter 6: Choosing Software). This means that you have to set up your client's database. Sometimes, databases are able to be converted from one software program to another, but don't count on this. You will likely have to input all the data yourself. This means that every superbill you receive will be a new patient for a while, even if it is not a new patient for the provider. You will need to work out a system with the provider and staff to ensure that you receive all demographic and insurance information for every patient that is seen for the first time since you took over as the billing service. This also means extra work for the staff. I am sure that coffee and scones or even lunch would be greatly appreciated by the staff for the extra work they will be expected to do on top of their regular duties to help you get started. I don't take the provider's entire database and enter every patient from that database into mine. I do it one patient at a time as they are seen. You may end up doing countless hours of unnecessary work if you attempt to input every patient the provider has had in the past year. There are a percentage of those people that will never be seen by your provider again. You don't want to waste your time doing unnecessary work. Focus on what will make you and your provider money. A process that I have found works well is to have the office staff attach a copy of the patient demographics and insurance to the charge slip. Once they have done this with a specific patient, then they should somehow mark the original demographic and insurance copies in the chart so everyone in the office knows that it was sent to the billing service, such as by marking a red X in the bottom right corner of the page. You could also offer to create new demographic intake forms for the office. By creating your own demographic intake, you will ensure all the information that you need is included on the form. If a new demographic intake is not in the chart, the staff will know to have the patient complete a new one and send a copy to you.

When considering your startup fee, you will want to take into account all the old account receivables the provider may have when you take over. Does the provider expect you to take over these old claims and patient balances? (Most likely, yes.) There will be rebilling to do, appeals, patient collections. You will also need to convert all the information into your database for these billings as well. Focus on the current paperwork the provider gives you first, but make sure to set aside a couple hours of the day to work on the old account receivables, and take it one patient, one claim at a time. See if you can find a way to print a report from the provider's old database showing you the aging claims. Work on them in order from oldest to newest, highest dollar amount to lowest. Many insurance companies have timelines within which you must submit claims in order to get paid. You want to make sure that you don't exceed these to get the most out of old account receivables. Then, you want to work on the simple correction rebills before you start on the appeals. Your focus is to get the provider as many old balances collected as possible as fast as possible. You may decide you want to use the provider's old database to work on these accounts. That will speed up the process if you think you can learn how to use the billing program quickly and sufficiently enough.

Considering all the factors listed above, you can now decide what method of startup fee you will charge. You can charge a flat rate startup fee or a percentage-based startup fee. A flat rate startup fee may be anywhere from three hundred to one thousand dollars depending on what old account receivables you are looking at. If you decide to charge a percentage on old account receivables, charge a higher rate than what you will charge the provider regularly. You don't know what kind of work you will have to get into, and you must be compensated for the work you will be doing. An acceptable percentage rate may be anywhere from 12 percent to 18 percent on the old account receivables. The provider is likely to not get a penny for the old balances if you are not willing to work on it, so a higher percentage should be easy to negotiate. You may remind the provider that a collection agency will take a much higher percentage—typically 35 percent to 55 percent. Even if you will not be working on old account receivables, I recommend that you negotiate for a flat rate startup fee, specifically for the time it will take setting up your database.

It can be difficult sometimes to collect on old patient balances. It can be time consuming, discouraging, and unprofitable. Figure out how much a statement costs: ink, paper, envelope, return envelope, stamp, and your time, which can become quite a costly item. Let's say it costs about three dollars total to send one patient statement. Then, take into account how many times you will send that statement without receiving a payment from the patient. That question can be answered by your agreed-upon amount in your contract, which is maybe two times. The cost of that statement total is now six dollars. Let's say you still don't get paid, and then you have to call the patient. This includes the cost of the phone call if long distance and your time; let's say it costs fifty cents. How many times do you make a phone call? Two times? The cost of the statement just went up to seven dollars. How much is the balance on that statement? One hundred dollars? If you are charging a percentage—let's say 8 percent—then your profit on that statement is now one dollar, if the patient pays. Not exactly worth it, right? Unfortunately, it's in your contract, and you have to do it. After your second phone call, you will probably give the bill to the provider's office and request it be sent to collections or be adjusted off. If it is sent to collections or adjusted, you might as well look at it as a seven-dollar loss to you. However, you may want to consider this option: telling the provider that you will take half your percentage for a staff-collected balance. So once you have put in as much time and effort as your contract states you will, then you can pass the balance along to the provider's office, and they can start to work on collecting it. The patient is more likely to call the provider's office back because they will assume that the call is in regard to an appointment or a lab. Then, the office will request the balance be paid and is more often successful because they can refuse to see the patient again until balances are paid. So the patient pays the balance, and you and the provider split the percentage. The patient paid one hundred dollars. Your percentage is now half of the usual, so you will receive four dollars for this balance collected. You will still be taking a loss, but the loss is only three dollars now instead of seven dollars, with no extra effort on your part.

Many providers give some sort of professional courtesy adjustments or bartering adjustments. The courtesy adjustments are usually for other providers and their families. I've seen providers barter for things such as strawberries, dental work, or construction. Unfortunately, you get nothing with these kinds of adjustments if the insurance doesn't pay! If an office visit is applied toward the patient's deductible, and the patient is a courtesy account, then you are expected to adjust the balance. In my contract, it is stated that if I bill the insurance and the provider wants to courtesy or barter adjust the balance, then they will still pay me the percentage I would have been paid for collecting the balance from the patient. I don't work for strawberries!

You will run into offices that have special circumstances, and you will need to find a fee solution. I would like to share a situation with you that took me some time to come up with a compromise on fees. I have one provider that is a certified nurse midwife. She is not in network with any insurance companies, so she does not have any contractual adjustments. If she bills forty-five hundred dollars for a delivery, then that's what she'll be paid between the insurance and the patient combined. Often, the insurance payments for a non-contracted provider will go to the patient. Then, the provider has to collect the balance from the patient. In this provider's case, she has the patient pay up front, and then anything that the insurance pays belongs to the patient. For a billing service, this can be a complicated situation. This type of medical billing involves a lot of follow-up and more extensive claim work. So I choose to be paid on a percentage basis rather than a flat fee per claim basis. Because the provider gets paid up front and the insurance pays the patient most of the time, it can complicate what the billing service charges the provider. I charge the provider a percentage based on the insurance allowable. Even though there are no contractual adjustments, the insurance still recommends adjustments on the explanation of benefits. So whatever the allowable is, whether it is paid to the provider, to the patient, or applied toward the deductible, I still get my percentage for that claims allowable.

You will want to be sure to have in your contract an "out" clause. If you and the provider decide to terminate the contract for any reason, given the amount of days' notice as defined in your contract, you will still need to be paid for the services that you provided up to the last day you entered and sent charges to the insurance company. There are several ways you can do this. You can trust the provider to track the payments that were billed by you and pay you as they are received. What you should do is define in your "out" clause that the provider will pay you your normal percentage of 50 percent to 70 percent of the account receivables outstanding your last day working on this provider's account. I have found that a provider gets paid on average 70 percent of what he or she bills out. This is about the same from insurance and patients. You will want to research and make changes as necessary to suit your area and provider.

You also will define in your contract penalties and fees for those situations, such as a finance charge for a late provider payment or fees for late or incomplete "Provider Responsibilities" as defined in the contract. With the software that I bill with, I have a station set up in each of my provider's offices for them to access the billing database for patient balances, patient information, and a scheduling program. I am unable to perform a system backup while someone at the office is logged into the database. I have stated in my contract that the offices are to log out of the database at the end of each business day. If that is not done, I impose a penalty fee against the office. If paperwork is supposed to be turned in to you on a specific day and it is not, there should be a penalty fee. Of course, you don't want to scare the provider away with too many penalties and fees, but you need to be in control of the billing, and you need to make sure the office knows that you mean business. You need the provider to perform his duties so you can perform yours. You may choose not impose the fees of a penalty on the first or even second occurrence, but be sure to let the office know that you are aware the mistake was made and in the future you will enforce the penalty fees.

All providers are different. Do as much research and background work as you can to make sure that you are getting paid what you deserve from your clients. Make the fee methods unique to your billing service and your clients. Just because you are getting one thing from one provider doesn't mean you can't get something completely different from another.

CHAPTER 6
CHOOSING
SOFTWARE

There are tens of thousands of medical billing software programs to choose from. It can be quite overwhelming unless you know what you are looking for. Some programs charge a monthly fee, and some you must purchase. The programs can cost anywhere from ninety-nine dollars per month to thousands of dollars to purchase. The cost of billing software does not make it a better or worse program. You just need to know what you are looking for and do all your research before choosing software.

If you Google "medical billing software," you will get more than twelve million website results. Like I said, a bit overwhelming, but it doesn't have to be. As always, the first page of a web search engine results list contains the most popular websites; this is a good starting point. Build yourself a questionnaire of points you want to know about each software program. You may choose to search the website for as many answers as you can find, or you can just call and ask all the questions. Be ready to be talk to a salesperson, though. They will most likely do anything to get your business and may continue to harass you if you give up any contact information to them. However, they can also be very knowledgeable and helpful to your research. Make sure you know whether you are dealing with a direct software vendor or a reseller; the pricing and details may differ from one to the other.

I would compile a list of questions of items that you would like to know about each software program. Go through the website, and see what questions you can answer that way. If you cannot answer them, you can give a salesperson a call. If any of the answers to your questions are unsatisfactory, then you can just scratch that software program off the list.

Below is a list of things you may want to consider while shopping for software program:

- Is the software for purchase or rent? If a rental, you will want to find out if there is a contract that includes a length of time to keep the software.

- Is the software web-based or an internal database? Find out what kind of backups there are in place for either.
    - If it's web-based, what happens when the website inevitably goes down or needs to close for maintenance? Are the times accommodating to the user?
    - If internal, who maintains the server? Do you have to pay additional IT support?
- Is the software capable of electronic and paper billing?
- What clearinghouse (discussed in detail later in this chapter) does the software work with, or can you chose which you want to work with?
- Does the purchase or rental price include updates? Your database will need to be updated regularly. The business of medical billing and the rules that go along with it are ever changing, as are HIPAA guidelines. There will be mandatory updates (which are for new laws and regulations) and arbitrary updates (non-law).
    - What is the additional price? Is it the same for both mandatory and arbitrary updates?
    - How often is the database updated? Is this done automatically, or do you need to request it?
- Does the software support multiple providers in separate databases? You may only have one client at first, but you do plan on growing your business and having multiple providers. You will need to have a separate database for each provider that you are working with. This ensures that you do not confuse one provider's patients with another's. You will also need to track the payments that come in by provider so you can bill the provider the services you have

rendered. Find out up to how many databases you can have and what the pricing is for each additional provider database you maintain.

- What kind of provider does the software support? The majority of software programs are tailored to common medical providers that bill in CMS 1500 forms. You will want to find out if they also support providers whose claims have special needs, like dentists, optometrists, podiatrists, or DME providers. You never know what specialty your business may expand into, so you will want to be ready for anything.
- What types of reports are offered? Are they customizable? Providers expect certain reports. They want to see what is going on with their charges and their payments. They want to see how fast their accounts receivable is being collected. Some providers want this monthly, some maybe weekly or even daily. You will need to make sure there are a variety of report options available because you won't know what your provider wants until you have him as a client. Some providers ask for pretty specific and not always common reports. You will want to know if the program will allow you to customize the reports.
- Does the software come with a CPT, HCPC and ICD-9/ICD-10 database, or will they all need to be entered by the user? This can be a tedious job if you have to enter it all into the database yourself. The idea that they would maintain it for you would normally come at an extra cost, I would expect. Coding books and websites are expensive, and I wouldn't expect anyone to give the new codes out for free. It would be nice if the database came with one initially, and you maintained it after that.
- How many computers can network and from how many locations?

o   Is the software multi-user or single-user? Some programs offer both. If you plan on growing your business, you may want employees and may want to upgrade to multi-user software. Find out the cost difference to upgrade.

o   Can the provider's office access the database? If needed, you could use remote desktop software for database access from multiple locations. You would need to have a PC available specifically for this, though.

o   Is there a scheduling program included for the provider? This would be a perk for the provider to use you as a billing service. It helps you track superbills, making sure that they get turned in, and alerts the staff if you have missing superbills that need to be turned in. It is also a good way to make sure the office sees patient balances to collect and for them to verify what information you have on the patient, should it need to be updated when the patient is in the office.

o   Is there an electronic medical records program that works with this software? Most offices have or will soon be converting to electronic medical records. Many electronic medical records programs come with billing software. It is not necessary for the two programs to work together. They work separately just fine, and I have found that most providers are OK with using two separate programs when the billing

53

service is maintaining the billing software.

- o Does this software offer eligibility verification? Provider's offices love this, and so will you once you work with them. It is an eligibility verification built in to the software. When the patient checks in and the superbill is printed, the eligibility is automatically verified by the software through the Internet. This feature is limited because not all insurance companies can verify online, but it is nice for the majority of the insurance companies that can. When you have to rely on the staff going to the specific insurance website or calling the insurance company and inevitably being on a minimum of a five-minute phone call, you may find yourself getting more denials for ineligibility. If you had a feature like this, if there was an eligibility issue, it would be resolved before the patient was provided any services.
- Is there technical support?
  - o Is it included in the purchase or rental price, or is it an additional cost? Some vendors offer free technical support; these would most likely be the ones that rent the software to you. But even then, some do charge for any technical support. You may find this varies when you are dealing with a reseller versus the software vendor directly. Some vendors charge outrageous prices for their technical support; that is why it is important to find out up front before

you decide you want to use their software. You want to make sure that your initial install will be supported and that any general questions you may have getting started are answered. Find out if there is a price you can pay for unlimited support for the entire year, though you want to make sure you will get your money's worth out of this. Find out what they charge hourly and if there is a minimum or initial charge for each instance.

o   What are the technical supports hours of operation? This is very important, too. You may start this business as a side job in addition to your regular job. If technical support is only open Monday through Friday, 8:00 a.m. to 5:00 p.m., then when will you be able to contact them if you need to? You want to be able to contact technical support when you need it, not when it's convenient for them. Consider their hours and yours.

- What are the computer system requirements? You want to make sure the computer that you have or will be purchasing supports the software.
- Can a provider's old database be converted into this software automatically? Sometimes this is possible, and it would be so convenient for you. You can cut costs on the startup fee if the programs are compatible. Make sure not to make any promises to the provider before you check with the software vendor on the provider's specific program compatibility.
- How long has the software company been in business? You don't want to invest time and money

55

into a company that will go out of business; make sure they are legitimate. Ask for references, local ones if possible, and call them. This will also get you started on networking.

- Is there training included?
  - o Can training be done before purchase and provider assignment? You probably wouldn't want to be paying a rental fee on software that you couldn't use without a client. It's sort of a catch-22. You want to be comfortable with the software and know how to use it, but you don't want to be paying for the software for months before you have a client. Some software programs can't even be set up before you have a provider.
  - o Does the software come with a user manual? Sounds like a silly question, but not all of them do. They may come with an online manual, which is fine. Ask if you can access it, and see if it seems detailed enough to use. Some may not offer manuals at all. This may be a way to get more money out of you through technical support.

Almost every software vendor out there has a trial version of their software that you can obtain either by mail or Internet download. I don't recommend paying for a trial version; they should always be free. I would question the validity of a company if they were to try to charge you for a copy of trial version software. I have also attended personal webinars with vendors to be given a tour of the software and ask questions as needed. I was given a username and password to enter the webinar, and after the webinar, I was able to access the demo version with my username and password to use and learn the software as I wanted.

I want to discuss reports further in detail. Reporting to your provider is very important. Prior to you being the billing service, the provider received reports on his billing. The provider is used to what he receives, how it looks, and when he receives it. You want to keep that as close to the same as possible—with improvements, of course. Ask the provider if you can obtain copies of the reports he regularly receives and note how often he receives these. You may know right off the bat if your software can generate these same reports. If the software does not, get to working on customizing a report so it does. You may find you are able to combine multiple reports into one. Ask if he is interested in any other reports that he does not already get. Offer ideas and samples of reports that you can generate from your software.

One common report that you will want to make sure your software is capable of generating is a production revenue report. This report will list each service, how many of each were billed in a specific time period, and a total dollar amount that was billed for each service. It may list by category with subtotals (billed amounts) and final totals, essentially giving the provider a total amount he has billed out for the time period and specifically what was billed out. It will also include a list of payments and adjustments. The payments should break out by insurance company. There should be a feature in your program that when you post payments, you post what service code they were paid for. This allows a report to generate, showing the provider what was paid for each specific code, allowing fee schedules to be verified. Most providers will want a short and to-the-point totals sheet. This will offer total charges entered, total payments, total adjustments, refunds, and ending accounts receivable for a specific time period. A provider will likely want to see each set of totals for a given time period to compare month to month on one page. Offering both long and short reports gives the provider an opportunity to quickly see how his or her numbers are looking and also offers him or her the ability to read in depth all the services being provided and paid for in his practice. It gives the provider a sense of understanding and control of the billing, making him or her more comfortable with the billing service.

Another common report providers want is an aging report. This report breaks down the accounts receivable to show how long it has been outstanding (e.g., 30 days, 60 days, 90 days, 120 days).

What is a clearinghouse? A clearinghouse is a centralized institution that collects, maintains, and distributes information. In the business of medical billing, a clearinghouse is used as a way to send electronic claims from your billing software to an insurance company. When you enter a charge slip into your billing software, you assign it an insurance company. A large number of today's insurance companies are able to accept electronic claims and provide a payer ID number. The payer ID number is a number assigned by a clearinghouse to the insurance company that tells the clearinghouse where to send the claim once you submit it from your billing software. At the end of the day when you run your claims to submit to the insurance companies, they are sorted into groups for each clearinghouse you use. The data is sent via modem or the Internet from your software in electronic format to the clearinghouse. At the clearinghouse, the claims are checked for accuracy, and possibly for eligibility, correct and current coding, HIPAA compliancy, and more. If the claims pass the clearinghouses tests, they are forwarded on to the individual insurance companies. If any claims did not pass the testing phase, they are reported back to the biller for correction and resubmission. Clearinghouses will offer a list of insurance companies that claims can be submitted to through them. Some of the larger insurance companies offer direct submission. These companies include Medicare, Medicaid, and Anthem Blue Cross of California. Submitting directly to the insurance company rather than through a clearinghouse has its advantages and disadvantages. The process of sending your claims may take longer, as you will be transmitting to each one individually. The customer support of a clearinghouse is often faster and more reliable than that of an insurance company.

There may be hidden costs to submitting direct, though they are free to transmit through; sometimes you must purchase additional software components.

You want to be able to choose your clearinghouse so that you are sure you are getting the fastest, most reliable company available for your clients. You want to select a company that caters to your client's specific needs and one that best fits your budget. You may use different clearinghouses for different providers. Hold on to your research on each clearinghouse you speak to. You never know when you might have a provider whose needs can be fulfilled by a clearinghouse that didn't work for another provider. There are not quite as many clearinghouses to choose from as there are medical billing software choices, but there are quite a few. Some important things to look for when choosing which clearinghouse to work with include:

- Carefully review the payer list. Make sure that the insurance companies that you regularly work with are included on that list.
- Contact the potential clearinghouse and inform them of which software you use. Ask if it is compatible and if they have other users of this software who are successfully submitting claims through them. Confirm with your software vendor as well.
- Ask if they are nationwide. You would rather work with a national clearinghouse than a regional one; it will offer more payers.
- Be knowledgeable of any contracts. Some clearinghouses want you to sign into a contract for a certain length of time. Look for ones that have month-to-month contracts if one is necessary.
- Contact customer support to get a feel for the time it will take to speak to a representative and the courtesy toward you.
- Ask to see what the error reports look like. Are they easy to read and have clear and concise rejection

details? Is the control center/website management easy to navigate and user friendly?

- Clearinghouses may charge a monthly unlimited submission fee, and some charge per claim and/or charge an initial setup fee. There are also clearinghouses that charge you only after you exceed a certain number of claims per month. This is nice if you are working with a small office that does not submit a lot of claims electronically. Watch out for additional costs. Some clearinghouses charge per provider or may charge an additional annual fee.
- How long does it take for them to report back to you about rejected or processed claims?
- Does the clearinghouse offer services such as electronic remittances or electronic funds transfer? Some will mail your paper claims for you and even send patient statements for you.

Even though you should be sending the majority of your claims electronically, you will still find some insurance companies that you cannot bill this way. You will need to keep CMS 1500 forms on hand at all times for submission of paper claims when necessary.

There are still provider's offices out there that do not bill electronically. This can be a great selling point to these providers, if you can find them. Getting an office set up to bill electronically should not be too difficult as long as you have good support through your software and clearinghouse. It will absolutely be worth your time to get the provider set up to bill electronically. The average clean claim billed through a clearinghouse takes on average three to sixteen days from the date submitted to the date a check is sent to the provider, versus a an average of twenty-eight days from receipt of a clean claim billed on paper to the insurance company for a check to be sent to the provider.

Another option a lot of insurance companies offer in addition to electronic claims submission is electronic remittance advice (ERA) and electronic funds transfer (EFT). Electronic remittance advice, also known as an explanation of benefits, can be downloaded via the clearinghouse to your software and/or for print. Some electronic remittance advice can also post directly to your software with the click of a mouse. Auto-posting takes compatibility between the clearinghouse and your software to function; this will save you time doing the data entry yourself. Electronic funds transfer means the insurance company directly deposits checks into the provider's bank account. This eliminates the mailing of the check from the insurance to the provider and the provider having to deposit the check in the bank. Electronic funds transfer makes the payments available in the provider's bank account in an average of fourteen days; it's faster and even less work for the provider than receiving the check by mail. I don't think you will find a provider that argues with that!

Choosing billing software is a very important part of starting your billing service. Take the time to research and think about your options. You want to feel comfortable using the software and know all the ins and outs of it. You want to be an expert at using it by the time you start working with your first client. It is, after all, your first attempt to show the provider what you can do for him or her.

CHAPTER 7
TRANSFER OF
PAPERWORK
FROM PROVIDER
TO YOU

The best part about choosing to start a medical billing service is that your clientele is limitless. You can have providers in multiple specialties and from anywhere. You can live in California and bill for a provider in Utah. You just need to be knowledgeable on the state laws on medical billing services and any state-funded insurance programs. While you are learning and growing your business, you may want to start a little smaller than that. As I said in an earlier chapter, choose a specialty, perfect it, and grow from there. The same thing goes for insurance companies. State Medicaid can be difficult to master, especially with this ever-changing industry.

Personally, I started my business because I live in a small town with limited job opportunities. I wanted to work from home so I could raise my children. One of my client's office is fifty miles from my house and an hour's drive. I certainly won't commute that far every day to obtain my paperwork. The provider and I worked out a system that worked for both of us. I travel to the provider's office once per week. The reason for this is not only because I need to pick up paperwork, but I also like for the office to know me. I pick up and drop off paperwork, and I also chat with the provider if he or she is available and allow him or time to discuss with me any questions or concerns. I do the same with the office staff. Occasionally, I bring along coffee and scones to spoil them a little. Can't hurt—these are the people whose efforts I need to make my work go more smoothly. I go on Tuesdays. If the office has a lot of paperwork on Thursday or Friday, they mail it to me in a prepaid, flat rate priority envelope, provided by me, the billing service.

A provider's office generally consists of the provider, an office manager, a bookkeeper or accountant, a front office person, a medical records clerk, and, depending on the type of provider, possibly nurses and/or medical assistants. I depend on all of these people to get the things I need to do the billing for the provider.

In this example, we will assume the provider is a general physician with an average-size practice. The front office staff maintains the scheduling and creates your superbills. They are the first contact between the office and the patient. I contact them when I am missing superbills that have been generated but not billed. The front office staff should review the insurance and patient demographic information and request payments of copayment and any outstanding balances on the patient's account.

The medical assistant or nurse will then take the superbill with the chart and put the patient into an exam room. I contact the medical assistant or nurse when I have questions regarding a visit. For instance, if a patient contacted me after I billed them for a coinsurance for a vaccine and stated that he or she never received that vaccine, I would contact the medical assistant or nurse to review the chart and determine if that was correct.

Then, the patient is seen by the physician. The physician completes the chart notes and the superbill. The front office person reviews the superbill to make sure it has been completed by the physician, removes it, and places it in a pile for billing.

The chart is then given to the medical records clerk, who files the chart note and the chart. If I need a chart note for appeals or because the insurance company requested it, I would request it from the medical records clerk.

The bookkeeper or accountant will obtain the mail and organize deposits for the billing service. Each check that is received by an insurance company should be copied and attached to the corresponding explanation of benefits. A list of the checks will be made on a deposit slip or ledger, and the corresponding explanation of benefits will be grouped together with that as a whole deposit. The accountant/bookkeeper will track all the payments for the month and be the one that you will need to balance all your deposits and month-end accounting totals with. He or she is also generally the person that receives and pays your bill at the end of each month.

Most of the time, the office manager is also one of the other mentioned employees, such as the accountant or nurse. The office manager is who you will need to contact if someone is not doing his or her job and it is directly affecting your ability to do your job as the billing service. The office manager may also be the person who coordinates the delivery of your paperwork.

Transfer of paperwork may be the reason you need a dedicated fax line. Many billing services have specific time slots for providers to fax in their paperwork on a daily basis. If you have multiple providers, then you would schedule each one of them a certain hour of the day to fax completed charge slips to you. I have found this does not work as well with deposits. The priority of your day should be charges; this is where the majority of the money is generated. You can receive the deposits another way and not necessarily as often as daily. Coordinating faxing can be a difficult task. The office staff assigned to the duty of faxing you paperwork may not always be available between 9:00 a.m. and 10:00 a.m. every day. What if they start faxing at 9:55 a.m., and another provider faxing for their 10:00 a.m. time slot cannot get through? This can be where penalty fees can be enforced as discussed in Chapter 5: Fees.

Fax may be a little outdated nowadays, and you may choose to have the office scan documents. But be careful to follow HIPAA guidelines when you transfer that paperwork. Confidentiality issues can arise when you are dealing with the Internet. The nice thing about scanning paperwork is that you save paper and can save money, depending on scanner purchase and maintenance. Plus, everything is saved as a document on your computer and can be later accessed much easier than pulling a file box from storage and going through it all by hand. It also eliminates your having to store all that paperwork and then return it a year later to the office for medical record storage.

The same cons are present for both faxing and scanning documents. It can be time consuming for the office if they have to remove staples from documents and store the scanned pages. The preparation may cause the delay of paperwork from the office to you to be greater than other methods. Most billing services request faxing or scanning to be a daily task.

Another way to receive paperwork, which is my preferred method, is by mail. You may be thinking, *What? Snail mail?* And the answer is yes. I provide each of my offices with prepaid, flat rate priority mail envelopes, enough to last them a full month. This requires the littlest effort on their part. They simply put the paperwork in the envelope, seal it, and put in the outgoing mail. Plus, I get all my paperwork at the same time—superbills, deposits, totals, and anything else. In the same state, it generally takes one day for me to receive the paperwork from the office. The provider is not paying to fax long distance and is not paying for the postage. I ask that the paperwork be sent twice per week at a minimum and more often if there is a full envelope.

You may find it helpful to review your provider's demographic intake sheet and any other forms that are required to be completed by the patients. There is certain information that you must have to bill medical insurance claims, and believe it or not, your provider may not ask for it on the demographic intake form. Even worse, they may have it and no one in the office pays attention to whether it all gets filled out. I receive intake forms from offices that are not signed or dated. I've seen missing dates of birth, illegible writing—things that should be caught and taken care of before the patient is even seen. Most providers include the assignment of benefits (AOB) statement on the end of their demographic intake form. The assignment of benefits is a legal statement allowing the provider to bill and receive funds from the insurance company on behalf of the patient. It also gives permission to share information about the patient's diagnosis and treatment with the billing service and insurance company. If the office does not have that statement, you cannot legally bill for services. I like to go over the demographic intake and the AOB statement to make sure everything I need is included and that it is also compliant. I remind the provider and staff regularly that the AOB statement signature must be updated yearly, and it is a good idea to just update everything yearly so that all the demographics are verified at least once a year in writing. If the demographic intake does not request all the information that you need, share with the provider what you need. You can offer to create a demographic intake that suits all your needs and that of the provider, or you can let the office create a new one. You will most likely have better luck making one for them, but you don't want to be pushy, either. Make sure you go over with the staff the importance of the required fields on the demographic intake and let them know the regulations about having the AOB statement signed yearly. You also need a HIPAA privacy form signed, discussed in detail in Chapter 9: HIPAA.

If a provider's office accepts insurance for things like automobile accidents, personal injury accidents, and/or workers' compensation, I like for them to have different intake forms for each of those specific cases. When you are dealing with automobile and workers' compensation insurance, the information that you need from the patient is much more specific for your insurance claim to be billed. I usually ask if the provider has a separate information request form for the patients to complete. If not, I ask if I can generate one so that all the specifics that I need will be provided by the patient. It can be quite a hassle if all you have are a company name and a patient's social security number. You may have to do a lot of calling around to get all the information you need. And generally, automobile and workers' compensation insurance companies are much more difficult to get paid from, and the turnaround time for a claim can be much longer. For a general practice that accepts mostly private insurance, state Medicaid, and Medicare, I generally recommend that they not accept any automobile or private injury cases. The reason is that with these insurance companies, generally there are two parties involved in a legal case of some sort. There will be a conclusion and perhaps a settlement at some point, but many of these cases take years to resolve. It is much smarter for the provider to require the patient to pay cash up front and provide the patient with the information necessary to file a claim themselves.

Even if the patient does have private health insurance, you must be careful. The patient may want you to bill his or her private insurance for a workers' compensation injury. Sometimes, they are dishonest and don't even tell you that it was a work-related injury. The private insurance company will come back later and recoup the money that they paid you if and when they find out it was a workers' compensation claim. This could happen years later, and you may never get the balance resolved. The patient may no longer be with your practice, and you may not be able to locate them to get the information that you need to bill the workers' compensation. Even if you did get a hold of the patient, it is not likely they still have that information or will get it for you. You of course cannot tell a provider who to bill and who not to; that is his choice. But you can recommend and suggest and give examples as to why, based on your past experiences and knowledge.

CHAPTER 8
INSURANCE
COMPANIES AND
PATIENT
COLLECTIONS

In this chapter, I will briefly discuss insurance companies. This book is not intended to instruct on how to do medical billing. This is a brief overview of some aspects of insurance and patient collections.

Insurance companies will do anything to hold on to their money as long as legally possible. The employee of an insurance company's job is not to pay you—it's to find reasons not to pay you. Or so it seems from a medical biller's perspective. You need to be an expert at dealing with insurance companies so that your providers get paid as fast as possible. In this chapter, I will share a few tricks of the trade with you.

Insurance companies are comprised of two major categories: private health insurance and public health insurance. Examples of public health insurance companies are Medicare, Medicaid, and other government insurance companies. Private insurance firms are mostly commercial companies, such as Anthem Blue Cross, Blue Shield, HealthNet, United Healthcare, Cigna, and Health Maintenance Organizations (HMOs), Preferred Provider Organizations (PPOs), Independent Physicians Associations (IPAs), and so on.

A provider can be participating or non-participating with any insurance company he or she chooses. Being a participating provider means the provider must accept the insurance company's guidelines and fee schedules for services rendered. The insurance company in turn lists the provider as a participating provider recommended to its consumers as a preferred provider. The insurance company offers higher fee schedules than non-participating providers, pays the provider directly, and processes claims more quickly. The patient is also more likely to use a participating provider because his or her out-of-pocket expenses will in most cases be less. Beware if you are working with a non-participating provider; the checks for your claims submitted may be sent directly to the patient instead of the provider. This can cause a great deal of frustration to a biller.

You must be fluent in medical insurance terminology. Familiarize yourself with common terms and definitions so that when you contact insurance companies, you will be able to better understand them and vice versa. You will need to know the difference between an HMO and a PPO, as well as definitions of copayments, coinsurances, deductibles, in-network, out-of-network, coordination of benefits, other health insurance coverage, and so on. A brief list of definitions and abbreviations is located in the appendix of this book.

Each insurance company has its own set of guidelines, especially if you are a participating provider. You must become familiar with these guidelines to ensure that you are getting the most and fastest reimbursement for your provider. Many insurance companies, both private and public, have websites. Not only can you verify eligibility and check claim status online, but in addition, most of these websites offer to send you bulletins and updates via mail or e-mail. You can also check the website's home page for recent updates. It is a good idea to keep as up to date as possible. With an insurance company like Medicaid, a rule can change from one month to the next with very little warning. If you are unaware of this change, it could result in a large number of denials, causing a delay in cash flow to your provider. As policies and procedures are constantly being updated, you will need to find the best way to keep on top of them.

As I said in Chapter 7: Transfer of Paperwork, it is very important to get all of a patient's demographic information for insurance claims. This includes information about the insured. When I say insured, I mean the person who is the primary subscriber of the plan. I find there are patients who do not understand this and that can complicate your insurance claim payment if it is billed incorrectly. Make sure you know who the insured is and who the dependents are. This is extremely important when a patient has multiple insurance companies so you can determine what the coordination of benefits is.

Often when you receive a denial from an insurance company that you believe is incorrect, you can call the insurance to have the claim reprocessed. This is the fastest way to get the claim reprocessed without having to send an appeal.

You would do this when you receive a denial for a duplicate or ineligibility when it was not a duplicate or the patient was eligible, or when the denial was the insurance company's mistake. It may take you some hold time to get to a customer service representative, but it eliminates the time for mail and will get paid faster. Remember to be confident when you are speaking to an insurance customer service representative. Be knowledgeable in what you are discussing and let him or her know who is in charge. If you are getting the runaround or the customer service representative seems like he or she doesn't know what he or she is talking about, it's probably because he or she doesn't. Don't hesitate to ask for a supervisor. Always get names of who you speak to and reference numbers if available. Make sure to get an approximate reprocessing time frame and follow up as close to that date as possible.

There are some tricks you can use when dealing with private insurance companies. They are the ones that will go to the extreme to not pay your provider. A private insurance company will deny claims wrongly, hoping that you will just write them off. They will process a claim incorrectly or only partially, hoping you will write the rest off because you didn't notice or didn't want to take the time to call them and wait on hold for fifteen minutes, only to be told you must submit your appeal in writing. So the following are tips that I have picked up along the way for dealing with these insurance companies, and hopefully, they will get you paid the first time.

When you must mail a paper claim instead of sending an electronic one, affix a brightly colored label to the top of the claim form that states: "If this claim is not paid or denied within thirty days, a formal complaint will be filed with the Insurance Commissioner." Claims that threaten the insurance company with the Insurance Commissioner will be given a higher priority and are less likely to "get lost" at the insurance company.

Sometimes, an insurance company will send you a letter requesting the patient's ID card. You know as well as the insurance knows that patient is eligible and they are just stalling to pay you. Send back the company's request with a request for your "additional information" charge. Inform the insurance that you would be happy to send them the requested additional information upon receipt of a thirty-five-dollar-minimum additional information fee. Most likely, the insurance company will process your initial claim and pay it.

If you are having trouble with a claim getting paid, it has gone repeatedly through the appeals process and not gotten anywhere, try involving the Insurance Commissioner. Honestly, you may not hear back from the Insurance Commissioner directly regarding your issue, but when you CC the insurance company a letter that you have sent to the Insurance Commissioner, they are more likely to pay attention and pay your claim before the Insurance Commissioner gets involved and could create a bigger problem for them altogether.

When you get a request from an insurance company for a recoupment of money that they paid you "in error," on their part, you do not have to refund it. If for some reason they did, however, overpay you legitimately, then you do. Let's say, for example, that the insurance paid you twice for the same service. You are obligated to refund them the overpaid money only. But if the insurance company states that they paid you incorrectly because of an error in eligibility on the company's part, then you do not have to refund them. Send them back the recoup request letter with your own letter stating that the request has been denied until the following documentation has been provided to justify the refund:

- A copy of the original claim submitted
- A copy of the paid cancelled check (endorsed by the payee)
- The reason for refund request
- A clear explanation as to why the original claim was paid and is now being denied
- A copy of the state statute of limitations in regard to refunds
- A copy of the section of the provider's contract that justifies the insurance company's entitlement to the refund request

Inform the insurance company that you are requesting this information from them in a timely manner and that the request for refund within fifteen days is unrealistic. Tell them that upon receipt of the documentation requested, you will review it to determine if a refund will be granted. Before you close your letter, make sure to state that you do not authorize recoupment from future payments from this insurance company to cover the refund, because if not, the insurance company will try to do so.

These are just a few simple tricks that I have picked up along the way that may help you get more money faster for your provider from the private insurance companies.

If your billing service includes patient statements and collections, be sure that you know all the laws in your state regarding patient collections. You will need to know the exact hours during the day that you can and cannot call, the laws regarding turning patients into a collection agency, insufficient funds laws, bankruptcy laws, and even when you take a patient balance to court. You also need to be clear with the provider on his or her preferences regarding patient balances and collections. You don't want to step on his or her patients' toes; make sure he or she is OK with the actions you are taking to collect balances and that he or she is also willing to allow you to follow through with your actions if and when necessary. The worst thing is when you tell a patient that he or she may not be seen at the office unless a balance is paid in full, and then he or she goes in and is seen without even paying that day's copayment. It puts the patient in control of the balance and says to the patient that he or she does not have to pay, ever.

It is with my experience that I say when you have a patient's work phone number, you are more likely to speak to that person and collect the balance. So many people have caller ID these days that your call can be easily avoided when you call a cell or home phone number. Make sure your patient demographic intake includes multiple contact numbers.

You want to be firm when calling patients for a past due balance. Let them know who you are, where you are calling from, and the balance, and tell them you would like them to take care of the balance by credit card today. Stay away from the patient "sob stories." If the patient tells you he or she just lost a job and his or her daughter just moved back in and the car has just been repossessed, tell the individual you are sorry to hear that and ask again that he or she pay the balance by credit card today. If he or she says it's impossible to pay the whole balance, ask to arrange a payment plan. Let the patient know that in order to be on the payment plan, he or she must make the first payment today by credit card. If the patient still refuses to pay today by credit card, then hold him or her to a date to pay by. Make a note to follow up with the patient the day he or she promised to pay to see that payment was indeed made. The best possible strategy to collect patient balances is to be consistent and follow-through. If the patient knows you are going to keep on him or her about a balance, he or she is more likely to pay.

Patient balances are a good reason to have the office staff capable of accessing your database. That is why I use software that includes a scheduling program that the office can use. They get the benefit of a scheduling program, and I am assisted with collecting the patient balances by the office. When the staff schedules an appointment with the patient, they can see if the patient has a balance and any notes regarding measures taken to collect that balance. With the provider's cooperation and approval, you can have the staff tell the patient that the balance is expected at the arrival of his or her appointment, and if the patient does not agree, he or she can contact the billing service. You can offer the provider a discount on the balances collected in this manner to entice him or her to let you train the staff on how they should collect this balance. Often, the balance is of less concern to your daily priorities because you will not make much of a profit from it. So if you offer the discount to the provider and get the staff to collect when patients come in, you will spend less time and effort on it, and the amount of profit you will make from it will not be dramatically affected.

You will gain knowledge and your own tricks of the trade with experience. Hopefully, this chapter will give you a head start. Joining a medical billing forum online can also be a great way to learn new techniques for dealing with insurance companies and patients. Be sure to share what you know with other billers as well.

CHAPTER 9
HIPAA: HEALTH INSURANCE PORTABILITY AND ACCOUNTABILITY ACT

The Health Insurance Portability and Accountability Act, or HIPAA, as you may know it better, was established in 1996. HIPAA protects personal health information under federal law. HIPAA privacy regulations were devised by the Department of Health and Human Services. Complete compliance was mandated on April 14, 2003. I remember taking my compliancy test for certification at the Wheelchair Center in 2003. Small businesses and insurance companies had until 2004 to be fully compliant.

HIPAA affects anyone who works with protected health information, including medical billing services, clearinghouses, shredding companies, copy services, software vendors, and more. The provider's offices, hospitals, and medical suppliers are considered "covered entities" under HIPAA regulations and are the most affected by its laws. The covered entities are the ones that provide you with the information you need to complete the medical billing. The covered entities must have a signed agreement with the patient to give this information to the billing service and must have a signed agreement with the billing service called a Business Associate Contract. Though there is still no standard contract that must be used, there are specific criteria that must be met. To review and comply with these criteria, refer to the HIPAA advisory website.

HIPAA laws are ever changing. I only briefly discuss HIPAA because the moment that I publish something about HIPAA, its accuracy could change. The main concern you have as a medical billing service in regard to HIPAA is to protect private health information. Use your common sense first and foremost. Don't leave any paperwork from your provider's office lying around the house for anyone to see. Don't throw away extra copies that you accidentally made; you must shred anything that contains protected health information. Verify who you are speaking with on the phone before you discuss private health information. You may not speak to anyone but the patient in regard to his or her own private health information. Permission to speak to anyone else must come from the patient themselves, verbally or in writing. Make sure that your office door is locked when you are not in it and that your file cabinets are locked. Put a password lock on your computer, and set a screensaver to lock your computer after a few minutes of inactivity. And no matter how interesting a patient encounter is, do not ever talk about patients to your friends and family.

HIPAA must be taken very seriously. Penalties for violation of HIPAA regulations start at fines of one hundred dollars and can be as high as two hundred fifty thousand dollars and even include jail time. Make sure you know and keep up with the current HIPAA laws. You are subject to the same penalties for inadvertently disclosing protected health information as you are for purposely disclosing it.

APPENDIX:
ABBREVIATIONS
GLOSSARY
FORMS

ABBREVIATIONS

AR:	Accounts Receivable
ABN:	Advance Beneficiary Notice
AOB:	Assignment of Benefits
CMS 1500:	Centers for Medicare and Medicaid Services Claim Form
CMS:	Centers for Medicare and Medicaid Services
COB:	Coordination of Benefits
CPA:	Certified Professional Accountant
CPT:	Current Procedural Terminology
DHHS:	Department of Health and Human Services
DME:	Durable Medical Equipment
DSL:	Digital Subscriber Line
EFT:	Electronic Funds Transfer
EMR:	Electronic Medical Record
EOB:	Explanation of Benefits
EOMB:	Explanation of Medical Benefits
ERA:	Electronic Remittance Advice
HCFA:	Health Care Financing Administration
HCPC:	Healthcare Common Procedure Coding System
HIPAA:	Health Insurance Portability and Accountability Act
HMO:	Health Maintenance Organization
ICD-10-CM:	International Classification of Diseases, 10th Edition, Clinical Modification
ICD-9-CM:	International Classification of Diseases, 9th Edition, Clinical Modification
IPA:	Independent Physicians Association
IT:	Information Technology
LLC:	Limited Liability Company
OHC:	Other Health Insurance Coverage
PC:	Personal Computer
PHI:	Protected Health Information
PPO:	Preferred Provider Organization
RAD:	Remittance Advice Details

W/O: Write-Off

GLOSSARY

Account Receivable (AR):	Money owed to a provider by its patients in exchange for services provided but not paid for.
Adjustment (aka Write-Off):	The difference between what is charged by the provider and what is allowed by the insurance company.
Advance Beneficiary Notice (ABN) (aka Waiver of Liability):	A form that Medicare requires providers to use to inform patients of services that Medicare does not or may not cover.
Allowable:	A maximum dollar reimbursement, as defined by an insurance company through a provider contract, for a specified service.
Assignment of Benefits (AOB):	Authorization from a patient, in the form of writing, to designate their medical benefits be paid to the provider on his or her behalf for services rendered by the provider.
Back Office Staff:	Office staff who deals with the administrative aspects of a company.
Batch of Payments (aka Deposit):	A collection of insurance checks and EOB's and/or patient checks compiled with a total dollar (deposit) amount to balance to.
Capitated:	A scheduled, fixed payment remitted to a provider, as part of a medical managed care program, for an enrolled patient.
Centers for Medicare and Medicaid Services (CMS):	Formerly known as Health Care Financing Administration (HCFA). A federal agency within the Department of Health and Human Services (DHHS). CMS administers the Medicare program and works in partnership with state governments to administer the Medicaid programs.

Charge Slip (aka Charges, Encounter, or Superbill):	An itemized form consisting of CPT, HCPC, and ICD-9-CM/ICD-10-CM codes. This form is completed by a provider to communicate services rendered to his or her biller.
Charges (aka Charge Slip, Encounter, or Superbill):	An itemized form consisting of CPT, HCPC, and ICD-9-CM/ICD-10-CM codes. This form is completed by a provider to communicate services rendered to his or her biller.
Clean Claim:	A complete and accurate claim, without errors, without need to obtain additional information.
Clearinghouse:	A centralized institution that collects, maintains, and distributes information.
Coinsurance:	A percentage-based out-of-pocket expense that the insured/patient pays for a specific medical service.
Coordination of Benefits (COB):	The method for determining which insurance company is responsible for primary payment processing when a patient has more than one insurance company.
Copayment:	A fixed out-of-pocket expense that the insured/patient pays for a specific medical service.
Corporation:	A company that is authorized to act and legally recognized as a single entity.
Covered Entities:	Any organization who directly works with personal protected health information.
Current Procedural Terminology (CPT):	A code set developed and maintained by the American Medical Association. This nationally used code set describes diagnostic, medical, and surgical procedures and services.
Data Entry:	The act of entering specific data into a software program for a specific purpose.

Deductible:	A specific out-of-pocket dollar amount that the insured/patient pays before his or her insurance company will pay for a service.
Dependent(s):	The spouse and/or children of the insured, as defined by the insurance company. Dependents may differ from one insurance company and/or state to another.
Deposit (aka Batch of Payments):	A collection of insurance checks and EOB's and/or patient checks compiled with a total dollar (deposit) amount to balance to.
Digital Subscriber Line (DSL):	High-speed, broadband Internet connection via telephone line.
Downcode:	To use a procedure code of a lower service value.
Durable Medical Equipment (DME):	Any medical equipment used in the home and to improve the quality of life, such as a wheelchair, hospital bed, nebulizer, and so on.
Electronic Medical Records (EMR):	A digital/computerized version of a person's medical record.
Electronic Remittance Advice (ERA):	An electronic version of an explanation of benefits.
Encounter (aka Charge Slip, Charges, or Superbill):	An itemized form consisting of CPT, HCPC, and ICD-9-CM/ICD-10-CM codes. This form is completed by a provider to communicate services rendered to his biller.
Explanation of Benefits (EOB) (aka Explanation of Medical Benefits (EOMB):	A document normally sent to both the provider and patient explaining the distribution of benefits for services billed by the provider.
Fee Schedule:	A list of fixed fees paid for specific

	services rendered by a healthcare provider as defined by a specific insurance company and its contract with that healthcare provider.
Front Office Staff:	Office staff who deals with patients and customers.
General Partnership:	An unincorporated company that is owned and run by two or more people.
Government Insurance:	Insurance provided by the federal government such as Medicare and Medicaid.
Health Insurance Portability and Accountability Act (HIPAA):	An act of Congress that set standards for privacy of protected health information, protection of health insurance coverage when changing jobs, and standards for electronic healthcare transactions.
Health Maintenance Organization (HMO):	A healthcare system that incorporates group practice, primary care physicians, and alternatives to traditional fee-for-service payment methods for providers, such as capitated payments.
Healthcare Common Procedure Coding System (HCPC):	Provides a standardized coding system to describe specific medical items and services for universal communication in the medical field.
Independent Physicians Association (IPA):	An association of independent physicians or organization contracting of independent physicians, providing services in a managed care organization.
Information Technology (IT):	Development, implementation, application, support, and/or management of a computer-based information system.
In-House:	To work in a provider's office as an employee.
In-Network Provider (aka	A healthcare provider that has a contract to be part of an insurance network.

Participating Provider):	Patients receive preferred rates and have less out-of-pocket expenses when using an in-network provider for their healthcare needs.
Insured (aka Primary Subscriber):	A person who owns insurance.
International Classification of Diseases (ICD):	A code set developed and maintained by the World Health Organization. This nationally used code set describes and sets diagnostic codes for classification of diseases.
Limited Liability Company (LLC):	A company that is a combination of characteristics of a corporation and a partnership or sole proprietorship.
Medicaid:	A federal health insurance system for qualifying low-income individuals, jointly funded by the federal and state governments, managed by each state individually.
Medicare:	A federal health insurance system for Americans age sixty-five and over and/or younger Americans with specific permanent disabilities or diseases.
Non-Participating Provider (aka Out-Of-Network Provider):	A healthcare provider that is not contracted to be part of an insurance network. Patients may pay more out-of-pocket when using an out-of-network provider for their healthcare needs.
Out-of-Network Provider (aka Non-Participating Provider):	A healthcare provider that is not contracted to be part of an insurance network. Patients may pay more out-of-pocket when using an out-of-network provider for their healthcare needs.
Out-of-Pocket Expense:	An expense that the insured/patient must pay directly to the provider as a result of services rendered, defined by

	the insurance company.
Participating Provider (aka In-Network Provider):	A healthcare provider that has a contract to be part of an insurance network. Patients receive preferred rates and have less out-of-pocket expenses when using an in-network provider for their healthcare needs.
Post or Posting:	To enter given data into a computer system.
Preferred Provider Organization (PPO):	A network of independent providers contracted with an insurance company to provide healthcare to the members of that insurance company at a discounted rate as defined by the insurance company.
Primary Subscriber (aka Insured):	Person who owns insurance.
Private health Insurance:	Funded by its members, private insurance is an alternative to government-run public health plans.
Protected Health Information (PHI):	Any part of an individual's medical record, including, but not limited to, health status, provision of healthcare, or payment for healthcare.
Provider:	A professional individual or healthcare organization that delivers health services or goods for payment.
Recoup:	To regain payments made in error.
Remittance Advice Details (RAD):	Notice and explanation of payment, adjustment, and denials listed on an explanation of benefits.
Sole Proprietorship:	A business that is owned and run by one person.
Superbill (aka Charge Slip/Charges or Encounter):	An itemized form consisting of CPT, HCPC, and ICD-9-CM/ICD-10-CM codes. This form is completed by a provider to communicate services rendered to his

	biller.
Upcode:	To use a procedure code of a higher service value.
Write-Off (aka Adjustment):	The difference between what is charged by the provider and what is allowed by the insurance company.

FORMS:
CMS-1500
PATIENT
REGISTRATION
FORM
SOFTWARE
QUESTIONNAIRE
SUPERBILL

CMS-1500

Patient Registration Form

DOCTOR M.D.
PATIENT REGISTRATION FORM

Today's Date:		

<table>
<tr><td colspan="3" align="center">PATIENT INFORMATION</td></tr>
<tr><td colspan="2">Patient's Full Name:</td><td>Marital Status:</td></tr>
<tr><td>Birthdate:</td><td>Age:</td><td>Gender:</td></tr>
<tr><td colspan="3">Address:</td></tr>
<tr><td>Social Security no.:</td><td>Home Phone no.:</td><td>Cell Phone no.:</td></tr>
<tr><td>Occupation:</td><td>Employer:</td><td>Employer Phone no.:</td></tr>
<tr><td colspan="3">Chose clinic because/referred to clinic by:</td></tr>
<tr><td colspan="3">Other family members seen here:</td></tr>
</table>

<table>
<tr><td colspan="5" align="center">INSURANCE INFORMATION</td></tr>
<tr><td>Person Responsible for Bill:</td><td>Birthdate:</td><td colspan="2">Address (if different):</td><td>Home Phone no.:</td></tr>
<tr><td colspan="2">Is this person a patient here?   Yes / No</td><td colspan="3">Is this patient covered by insurance?   Yes / No</td></tr>
<tr><td>Occupation:</td><td>Employer:</td><td colspan="2">Employer Address:</td><td>Employer Phone no.:</td></tr>
<tr><td colspan="5">Please indicate primary insurance:</td></tr>
<tr><td>Subscriber's Name:</td><td>Subscriber's S.S. no.:</td><td>Birthdate:</td><td>Group No.:</td><td>Policy No.: Co-Payment: $</td></tr>
<tr><td colspan="5">Patient's Relationship to Subscriber:</td></tr>
<tr><td colspan="5">Name of Secondary Insurance (if applicable):</td></tr>
<tr><td>Subscriber's Name:</td><td>Subscriber's S.S. no.:</td><td>Birthdate:</td><td>Group No.:</td><td>Policy No.: Co-Payment: $</td></tr>
</table>

<table>
<tr><td colspan="4" align="center">IN CASE OF EMERGENCY</td></tr>
<tr><td>Name of local friend or relative (not living at same address):</td><td>Relationship:</td><td>Home Phone:</td><td>Work Phone:</td></tr>
</table>

The above information is true to the best of my knowledge. I authorize my insurance benefits to be paid directly to the physician. I understand that I am financially responsible for any balance. I also authorize my insurance company to relase any information required to process my claims.

Patient/Guardian Signature	Date

Software Questionnaire

Name: Website:
Phone: Contact:

Software purchase/rent:
$

Electronic claims: per claim/per month
$

Tech Support: Included/per hour
$

Tech support hours of operation:

Software updates: Included/additional cost
$

Statements: By program/by owner
$

System requirements:

Training:
Can training be done before purchase/provider assignment?
$

Scheduling and/or EMR software included/additional:
$

Networking: How many computers can network?

Multiple providers:
$

Superbill

Office Visit	New	Estab.	Laboratory		Injections	
Minimal	99201	99211	ALT/SGPT Alanine	84460	Admin	95115
Brief	99202	99212	Glucose	82962	B-12	J3420
Limited	99203	99213	Guaic	82270	Ceftriaxone	J0696
Intermediate	99204	99214	Hemoglobin (A1C)	83036	Kenalog	J3301
Comprehensive	99205	99215	Hemoglobin (Hgb)	85018	Toradol	J1885
Home-Low	99342	99348	Lipid Panel	80061		
Home-Mod	99343	99349	Pregnancy Test	81025	**Immunizations**	
Home-High	99344	99350	Prothrombin Time	85610	Admin	
			Rapid Flu	87400	Adacel/Tdap	90715
Preventative			Rapid Strep	87081	DTAP	90700
Under 1 Year	99381	99391	Specimen Handling	99000	Flumist	90660
1-4 years	99382	99392	Urine Dip	81002	Gardasil	90649
5-11 years	99383	99393	Urine Micro	81000	Hepatitis B Ped/Adol.	90744
12-17 years	99384	99394	**Office Procedures**		Hepatitis B Adult	90746
18-39 years	99385	99395	Anoscopy	46600	HIB	90645
40-64 years	99386	99396	Audiometry	92552	Influenza Adult	90658
65+ years	99387	99397	Bronchodilation Resp.	94060	Influenza >3 yr PF	90656
			Ear Irrigation	69210	Influenza 6-35 mo.	90657
Office Supplies			EKG & report	93000	Influenza 6-35 mo. PF	90655
Ace Wrap	A4465		Inhalation Therapy	94640	IPV/Polio	90713
Cast Supplies	A4580		Pulse Ox	94760	MMR	90707
Cath Kit-Male	A4326		Pulse Ox Multi	94761	Pentacel	90698
Cath Kit-Female	A4328		Resp. Flow Vol. Loop	94375	Pneumococcal	90732
Dressing	A6251		Spirometry	94010	PPD	86580
Supplies/Materials	99070		Treadmill	93015	Prevnar 13	90670
Surg. Supply, Misc	A4649		Tympanogram	92567	Varicella	90716
Surg. Tray	A4450		Vision Screen	99173		

DIAGNOSIS

Abscess	682.9	Coagulopathy	286.9	Feeding Problem	783.3	Knee Derangement	717.9	Proteinuria	791.0
Abdominal Pain	789.00	Colon Irrit. IBS	564.1	Fever	780.60	Knee Sprain	844.9	Rash	782.1
Acne	706.1	Concussion	850.9	Fibrocystic Breast	610.9	Laryngitis	464.0	Rectal Bleed	569.3
Allergic Rhinitis	477.9	Conjunctivitis	372.30	Fifth Dz	057.0	Lipoma	214.9	Rotator Cuff Dz	726.10
Allergy to:	693.	COPD	496	Flu	487.1	Low Back Pain	724.2	Scabies	133.0
Alzheimers	331.0	Constipation	564.00	Urinary Frequency	788.41	LS Strain	846.0	Seb. Cyst	706.2
Amenorrhea	626.0	Cough	786.2	Ganglion	727.49	Lymphadenopathy	785.6	Seizure Dis.	780.39
Anemia	280.9	Croup	464.4	Gastritis	535.00	Menopause	626.9	Sciatica	724.3
Angina	413.9	Dehydration	276.51	Gastroenteritis	558.9	Menses Irregular	626.4	Sinusitis	461.9
Ankle Sprain	845.00	Dental Caries	521.00	GERD	530.81	Migraine	346.10	SOB	786.09
Anxiety	300.00	Depression	311	GI Bleed	578.9	Molluscum Contag.	078.0	Strep Throat	034.0
Arrhythmia	427.9	Dehydration	276.51	Goiter	240.9	Mononucleosis	075	Stroke	436
Arthritis Gen.	716.90	Dermatitis	691.8	Gout	274.9	Muscle Spasm	728.85	Suture Removal	V58.31
Arthritis Osteo.	715.00	Derm. Diaper	691.0	Glossitis	529.0	Myalgia/Myosite	729.1	Syncope	780.2
Arthritis Rheum.	714.0	Derm. Seb.	690.10	Glucose Intol.	271.3	Onychomycosis	110.1	Tachycardia	785.0
Asthma	493.93	Diabetes .00, .02	250.	Headache	784.0	Obesity	278.00	Tendonitis	726.90
Atrial Fibrillation	427.31	Diarrhea	787.91	Heart Murmur	785.2	Obs. Sleep Apnea	327.23	TIA	435.9
Back Ache	724.5	Disc Disease	722.6	Hematuria	599.70	OME	381.10	Tinea	110.9
Bacterial Rhinitis	460	Diverticular Dz	562.00	Hemorrhoids	455.6	Osteoporosis	733.01	Tonsillitis	463
BPH	600.00	DVT	453.9	Hypercholesterol	272.0	Otitis Externa	380.10	Ulcer Skin	707.00
Breast Mass	611.72	Dyspepsia	536.8	Hypogonadism	257.2	Otitis Media	382.9	URI	465.9
Bronchiolitis	466.19	Dyspnea	786.09	Hyperlipidemia	272.2	Otalgia	388.70	Urticartia	708.9
Bronchitis	466.0	Dysuria	788.1	Hypertension	401.9	Palpitations	785.1	Urethritis	597.80
Bursitis	727.3	Edema	782.3	Hyperthyroidism	242.90	Panic Attack	300.01	UTI	599.0
CAD	414.00	Elev. Blood Press.	796.2	Hypothyroidism	244.9	Parkinson's Dz	332.0	Vaginitis	616.10
Candida Derm.	112.9	Emesis	787.03	Immunize Update	V03.9	Paronychia Finger	681.02	Varicose Veins	454.9
Carpal Tunnel Syn.	354.0	Enuresis	788.36	Incontinence Stool	787.60	Paronychia Toe	681.11	Venous Insuff.	459.81
Cellulitis	682.9	Epididymitis	604.90	Incontinence Urine	788.30	Peptic Ulcer	533.90	Vertigo/Dizziness	780.4
Cerum Impact	380.4	Epistaxis	784.7	Ingrown Toenail	703.0	PVD/PAD	443.9	Viral Synd.	079.99
Cervical Sprain	847.0	Erectile Dysf.	607.84	Insomnia	780.52	Pharyngitis	462	Vitamin B-12 Def.	281.1
Chest Pain	786.59	Esophagitis	530.10	Intertrigo	695.89	Phlebitis	451.9	Vitamin D Def.	268.9
CHF	428.0	Exanthem	782.1	Jaundice	774.6	Pneumonia	486	Vomiting	787.03
Cholelithiasis	574.00	Fail to Thrive	783.41	Keratosis Actinic	702.0	Prostatitis	601.0	Warts	078.10
Chondromalacia	733.92	Fatigue	780.79	Keratosis Seb.	702.19	Prost. Hypertrop.	600.00	Zoster	053.9

Notes:

Made in the USA
San Bernardino, CA
09 November 2016